OUR LEGENDS

OUR LEGENDS

Luminaries Who Revived Islam

By

Mufti Abdul Wahab Waheed

&

Mustafa Rasheed

KUBE PUBLISHING

In association with

مفتاح
MIFTAAH INSTITUTE

Our Legends: Luminaries who Revived Islam

First published in England by
Kube Publishing Ltd
Markfield Conference Centre,
Ratby Lane, Markfield,
Leicestershire, LE67 9SY,
United Kingdom
Tel: +44 (0) 1530 249230
Fax: +44 (0) 1530 249656
Email: info@ kubepublishing.com
Website: www.kubepublishing.com

cip data for this book is available from the British Library.

ISBN: 978-1-84774-154-9 *paperback*
ISBN: 978-1-84774-155-4 *ebook*

Cover Design by: Jannah Haque
Typesetting by: nqaddoura@hotmail.com
Printed by: Elma Basim, Turkey

DEDICATION

This book is dedicated in loving memory of my beloved and honourable younger brother, Shaheed Shaykh Abdul Raheem Waheed رحمه الله. May Allah سبحانه وتعالى continue to elevate your ranks! *Ameen*

(Mufti Muhammad Abdul Wahab Waheed)

بسم الله الرحمن الرحيم

CONTENTS

TRANSLITERATION TABLE

Arabic Consonants

Initial, unexpressed medial and final: ء ’

ا	a	د	d	ض	ḍ	ك	k
ب	b	ذ	dh	ط	ṭ	ل	l
ت	t	ر	r	ظ	ẓ	م	m
ث	th	ز	z	ع	‘	ن	n
ج	j	س	s	غ	gh	هـ	h
ح	ḥ	ش	sh	ف	f	و	w
خ	kh	ص	ṣ	ق	q	ي	y

With a *shaddah*, both medial and final consonants are doubled.

Vowels, diphthongs, etc.

Short:	ـَ	a	ـِ	i	ـُ	u
Long:	ـَا	ā	ـِي	ī	ـُو	ū
Diphthongs:			ـَوْ	aw		
			ـَيْ	ay		

PREFACE

Mufti Muhammad Abdul Wahab Waheed

IT IS TRULY from the *Tawfīq* of Allah Most High that He has allowed me to undertake and complete this project. To be able to speak and write about the great figures that are compiled in this book was truly an honour and privilege. There have been many individuals who have studied and elucidated the lives of influential entrepreneurs, philanthropists, historians, inventors and others who have left an impact on this world. However, I am certain that no study is more enjoyable and beneficial than that of the lives of those who become a source of motivation for earning the pleasure of and nearness to Allah Most High. It would be a disservice to their sacrifices if we did not make an attempt to learn about their unwavering dedication and commitment to this beautiful *Dīn*. Hence, in 2018, I began this journey and made it my mission to summarize their lives and share it with my students. I then decided to make a short video series on their lives on the advice of many friends and colleagues who felt it would be beneficial for others. Thereafter, I reached out to Mustafa Rasheed to help me summarize my videos into articles and publish them on our Miftaah website. After completing a few of these articles, I realized that it would be a better idea to these as a book.

The objective of this book is not just shedding light on people who left their mark on this world, but rather to make us amongst the chosen slaves of Allah who are able to effect spiritual and societal changes.

Inshā'Allāh I will continue to add different personalities to this work. In the future, I hope to include female pioneers or dedicate a whole book to them. All of the individuals included in this book possessed numerous great qualities, but all of them shared three common traits. My goal throughout this book was to highlight briefly these three qualities.

The first quality is sacrifice. All these personalities were always ready to put aside their personal needs and ulterior motives to ensure that the *Dīn* of Allah Most High thrives. Success at any level comes with sacrifice and, without sacrifice, one will struggle to achieve any success. People make all kinds of sacrifices to secure a better life. The difference between most Muslims todays and the figures mentioned in this book is that their sacrifice was for the sake of preserving the *Dīn* and making it progress. Therefore, one needs to make a firm intention that one's progress and one's family progress are for the sake of the progress of one's relationship with Allah Most High. Once this relationship progresses, everything else in one's life will also grow and advance. In order for this beautiful religion and way of life to touch the lives of others, we must raise the bar of how much we are ready to give up for the sake of Allah Most High.

The second quality is selflessness. Modern society inculcates selfishness. Our righteous predecessors were constantly worried and concerned about the well-being of others. The Prophet (blessings and peace be upon him) taught us that the best amongst us all are those who can bring more benefit to others. This does not simply imply that one shows altruism towards others with regard to food, water and shelter, it also means that one should want for others whatever blessing one has, and the greatest blessing one has is Islam. It would be selfish of us to want Islam just for ourselves. We should use our careers and talents to lead people to the beauty of our religion. Using one's talent to benefit oneself is great, but using it to bring benefit and goodness to others is the true goal. The great personalities studied in the present book were aware of their talents, they fine-tuned them, and then used them to bring benefit to others. The best way to use one's time and energy is to bring people closer to Allah Most High.

The third and last quality is the ability to assimilate into society while setting aside a certain time with Allah Most High, i.e. keeping a balance between social work and deep-rooted acts of devotion. Sometimes, one can be immersed in personal acts of worship without using the strength that comes from that to support the voiceless. On the flip side, one can be involved in supporting others and working for the community without having a personal relationship with Allah. This is why the Prophet (blessings and peace be upon him) was told to work for the community but without neglecting his *Tahajjud*. The worship of the night is what gives power to the efforts and endeavours of the day. Social work should not come at the expense of personal spiritual growth, and vice versa.

I conclude my preface with a heavy heart and with tears streaming down my cheeks. Not only because Allah ﷻ allowed me to be a part of this project, as I am not worthy of it, but also because I wish my younger brother was able to see this project completed. The chapters of this book were completed before the worldly departure of my dear beloved younger brother, Shaykh Abdul Raheem رحمه الله. I was not able to include a chapter for him, and perhaps that is for the best so I can dedicate an entire book for his short, yet influential life. He lived in this worldly life just 22 years but his impact continues to touch thousands of people. I pray to Allah Most High that He grants the reward of this project to my dear brother. He will be the greatest source of motivation for me after Allah Most High and the Prophet (blessings and peace be upon him) for any and every project that I am allowed to be a part of. I ask you all to pray for him and all the other great legends spoken about in this book.

Lastly, I would like to thank those without whom this project would not have been possible. I start with my beloved and respected father, the greatest human being I have ever met and sat with; a man who has sacrificed more for the *Dīn* of his children than words can describe. I only pray that one day my brothers and I can also be like you. Secondly, I thank the heartbeat of my life, my beloved and honourable mother; a mother like none other. Without her prayers and smile, I do not think any of our endeavours would have beeen possible. Thirdly, I would like to thank my dear and respected brothers, Shaykh Abdullah Waheed, Mufti Abdul Rahman Waheed, Shaykh Dr. Abdul Aziz Waheed, and Shaykh Shaheed Abdul Raheem Waheed ﵀, who continue to directly and indirectly mould me. Without their love and encouragement, these projects would be fruitless, and without their guidance and inspiration, I would not be able to put ink to paper. I also thank my wife for her understanding and unwavering support, and thank my sisters-in-law, nephews and nieces for the happiness they bring to my life. I hope that one day they can also read this book and benefit from it. I would also like to thank all of my students at Michigan Islamic Institute for their love and support. It was them who first motivated me to begin this project. I would also like to express my appreciation to my dear friend and student Hasan Suleiman, who helped me complete this project at every level. I could not finish my acknowledgements without expressing my gratitude to my fellow author Mustafa Rasheed. Without his support and contribution, this project would not have been possible. Lastly I would also like to acknowledge all of my teachers who enabled us to be part of this family of knowledge, starting with Dr Abdul Razzaq Sikandar ﵀, Mufti Abdul Majeed Dinpuri Sahib ﵀, Shaykh Fadhl Muhammad, Mufti Abdul Raoof Ghaznawi, Mufti Abdul Majid, Mufti Aasim Rashid, and many others who would prefer not be mentioned by name.

Lastly, I would like to thank Allah Most High for this opportunity and I also ask Him to continue using us for the service of His *Dīn*. We have no power or ability, everything comes from Allah Most High. May Allah accept this project and make it a source of benefit for the whole Ummah; and may Allah's blessings and peace be upon the greatest of creation, our Beloved Prophet Muhammad.

PREFACE

Mustafa Rasheed

ALL PRAISE and thanks are due to Allah ﷻ, the Sovereign, the All-Knowing, and the Protecting Friend. I bear witness that there is none worthy of worship except Allah ﷻ and that Muhammad, may peace and blessings be upon him, is His Messenger.

In mid-2018, Miftaah Institute produced an online video series entitled *Saviors of Islam* where Mufti Muhammad Abdul Wahab Waheed, the co-founder and director of Miftaah Institute, expounded on the lives of the great revivers of the Muslim *Ummah*. Br. Niyaz Uddin, the Institute's creative director at the time, knew I was an amateur researcher and writer, and therefore, asked me to draft articles on each of the personalities in the series. The idea was that if the viewers wished to learn more, they could use these extended biographies as a resource. I published several articles over the next eight months, trying to cover each of the personalities in the series. Approximately one year later, Mufti Abdul Wahab suggested changing the trajectory of the project. We would continue to produce more biographies and improve the ones we had already published, eventually compiling them into a book for the benefit of the public. Mufti Abdul Wahab directed the project's general vision, supplied the text with translations from Arabic sources, and offered some added commentary. My responsibility was to finalize the manuscript, a two-year writing process of infusing my own historical research and writing with Mufti Abdul Wahab's material into a comprehensive narrative. Several drafts later, we collaborated over a multitude of editing sessions to come up with this final draft.

The text before you, *Our Legends*, is a biographical compilation of ten luminary figures of the Islamic tradition. ʿUmar ibn ʿAbd al-ʿAzīz ﷺ and Ḥasan al-Baṣrī ﷺ are precedent-setters of the religion's earliest generations. Imam Abū Ḥanīfah ﷺ, Imam al-Shāfiʿī ﷺ, Imam Aḥmad ibn Ḥanbal ﷺ, Imam al-Bukhārī ﷺ, and Imam al-Nawawī ﷺ were highlighted for their contributions to the codification of Islamic jurisprudence and Hadith. We felt Ṣalāḥ al-Dīn al-Ayyūbī's ﷺ unique station as a pious world leader was a welcome addition to our academic ensemble of profiles. The final inclusions of Shāh Wallīullāh ﷺ and Mawlana Anwar Shāh Kashmīrī's ﷺ were added to represent scholarship in the Subcontinental colonial era and provide a humble nod to Mufti Abdul Wahab's pedagogical heritage. We envisioned this text to blend academic biographical writing with inspirational narratives like uplifting quotes and general advice. It has a historical quality while also elucidating values and lessons with the appropriate Arabic to draw inspiration from. Each chapter is short and concise in comparison to other works. While it is a fantastic resource for familiarizing oneself with history, it does not go into extraordinary depth nor offer extensive critical analysis. It is a text where I hope readers will gain a basic understanding of each personality and a means to draw spiritual benefit.

I wish to share three lessons I learned in the course of writing this book. First, the scholars and saints we discuss here were symbols of balance. Today, when Muslims seek knowledge, they are susceptible to falling into two wayward camps. They can become people who learn a few aspects of the *Dīn* and then immediately point fingers and classify people as "the other". On the other hand, when some attain knowledge, they withdraw to their homes and see any interaction with society, particularly the parts they are uncomfortable with, as a guaranteed corruption of the heart. The figures of the past mentioned in this book were always engaged with their communities. Yes, there are rulings one must adhere to, acts to avoid, people one should be wary of, and other things to be done. Nevertheless, the Muslim *Ummah* is founded on mercy, tolerance and understanding. The pious of the past interacted with the public and crossed paths with the lowest and disliked elements of society. They were not offended or accusatory. Rather, it was their mercy and tolerance towards others that attracted people to them and Islam. When one is involved in the public sphere, particularly in the West where identity labelling and unhealthy polemics is rampant, Muslims should impart an attitude of positivity. The real scholars and teachers of others are the ones who make life easier for others but are very strict with themselves.

The second lesson is the necessity of recognizing the never-ending challenge of adjusting and correcting oneself and one's society in order to adhere to the spirit and letter of the message to our beloved Messenger ﷺ. Unfortunately, many elements in the Muslim *Ummah* maintain a dogmatic inclination to generational attitudes and practices. They try to replicate an identical zeitgeist of Islam practised by past generations, without any consideration for cultural shifts. Undoubtedly, Islamic history and traditions contain a richness of experiences and benefits that should be respected and deeply analysed. However, one honours the Islamic tradition because it was constantly being enriched by forward and critical thinking scholarship in order to reorient different generations and cultures to the message of Islam. While the *Sharīʿah* and the spirit of Islam are universal in time and space, each generation and culture must be stimulated to honour that universality in the way that works best for them. Imam al-Bukhārī ؒ and Mawlana Anwar Shāh Kashmīrī ؒ were not symbols of an identical, uncompromising mind-set. They and all those like them challenged the status quo to improve and restructure their society to adhere to the principles of Islam. What worked in one community may not work in another and that is perfectly acceptable as long as what is being adopted is not contrary to the *Sharīʿah*. It is possible to be diverse, change and improve without sacrificing the *Sharīʿah* of Allah ﷻ. Tolerance and compassion in the face of differences were traits that were symbolic of the Prophet ﷺ and his heirs.

The third lesson is about women. Many of these great scholars would not have reached the status they had reached if it were not for their mothers who put the love of Islam in their hearts. The love that invigorates students to become major contributors to Islamic scholarship and asceticism comes from the mother. I regret that this edition of the book was not able to discuss the lives of exceptional women who raised the intellectual and spiritual standard of this *Dīn* and pray that writers more capable than me highlight this aspect of Islamic scholarship. Today, under the excuses of modesty and privacy, women are not adequately accommodated in Muslim centres of learning. Muslims must make people feel safe in their spaces so they can focus on perfecting their relationship with Allah ﷻ. As an *Ummah*, Muslims must raise their standards such that the only distinguishing feature between humans is what lies in their hearts when they stand before Allah ﷻ and their deeds are evaluated. This includes a greater effort to take care of orphans and the impoverished, something that many of our great predecessors did. I ask Allah ﷻ that not only will this book be a source of history but also a source of change, both inwardly and outwardly.

I take this opportunity to acknowledge and thank my family for their support, particularly my parents Drs Abdur and Zehra Rasheed. A special thanks to Rexhinaldo Nazarko, Bashaar Shah, Niyaz Uddin, and Zehn Wani for their support. Saim Rehman and Faraz Ansari provided a fresh set of eyes to my drafts and gave me a renewed insight into writing.

It is the *Sunnah* of Allah ﷻ that He executes His will through natural means, which only serves to strengthen the faith of those who observe these signs and ponder over them. History reveals that in Islam's darkest times, this religion was safeguarded through righteous individuals who upheld Islam in its truest sense. They stood as pillars with their qualities of sacrifice, unwavering faith, morality and intellect. We find that despite the repeated attacks faced by Muslims, the *Ummah* always persevered. By the will of Allah ﷻ, it will continue to do so, as long as individuals continue to hold fast to their *Dīn* and follow the examples of those who suffered and triumphed before.

عمر ابن عبد العزيز

ʿUmar ibn ʿAbd al-ʿAzīz

The Fifth Rightly-Guided Caliph

INTRODUCTION

FOR MANY, initiating concrete and drastic change conjures up apprehension and a sense of fear of the unknown. However, ʿUmar ibn ʿAbd al-ʿAzīz's ﷀ vision of change was not hampered by such anxieties, as for him it was a persistent and ever living reality. He understood that change must begin with himself even if it meant sacrificing his own privileges and comfort for the sake of the well-being of his people. This norm was first revived by our beloved Prophet Muhammad ﷺ, an honourable and revered individual who made the interests and benefits of others his greatest goal in life. The Prophet ﷺ said:

أَحَبُّ النَّاسِ إِلَى اللهِ أَنْفَعُهُمْ لِلنَّاسِ

'The most beloved people to Allah are those who are most beneficial to others.'[1]

This norm of putting first the interests and benefits of others was continued during the reigns of the four leaders of the Muslim Ummah after the Prophet ﷺ. It was, however, discarded by the first Umayyad rulers until it was restored again by the great 'Umar ibn 'Abd al-'Azīz ﷺ.

EARLY LIFE AND APPOINTMENT AS CALIPH

'Umar ibn 'Abd al-'Azīz ﷺ was born in Madinah in 63 AH/682 CE. His mother, Umm 'Āṣim was the granddaughter of 'Umar ibn al-Khaṭṭāb ﷺ, the second Rightly-guided caliph. It was one of the night habits of 'Umar ibn al-Khaṭṭāb ﷺ to walk around the streets of Madinah to inspect the affairs of his subjects. It is narrated that in one such nightly inspections, he overheard a poor woman asking her daughter to mix milk with water, which is forbidden in Islam. The girl, however refused to comply with her mother's demand. The mother urged her to do it because the Caliph was not present and would never find out about it. The daughter replied that even if the Caliph was not present, Allah Most High, who is All-Seeing, was surely watching them. Such was the level of *taqwā* and God-consciousness of this young woman.

One often feels that one's hidden deeds are limited in their effects and magnitude because no one sees them or knows about them. However, the Qur'an and the Prophetic Sunnah teach us that the deeds that one hides from others have the greatest consequences and impact.

No human being saw Hājar when she was hurrying between the mountains of Ṣafā and Marwah but since the ordination of the Pilgrimage (*Ḥajj*), every single Muslim pilgrim has to walk and run between those two hillocks as part of the rituals of *Ḥajj*. The story of this young woman conveys the same thing.

Impressed by this girl's reply, 'Umar ibn al-Khaṭṭāb, asked his sons, upon returning from his inspection, whether any of them wished to marry this girl. His son 'Āṣim, agreed to marry her. From this blessed marriage, a daughter, Laylā bint 'Āṣim, was born. When this daughter was of age, she married someone from the Umayyad clan, 'Abd al-'Azīz ibn Marwān, and 'Umar ibn 'Abd al-'Azīz was born from this marriage.

'Umar ibn 'Abd al-'Azīz grew up in Egypt where his father was governor and remained there until his father's death. He also spent part of his youth in the Holy city of Madinah, of which he would later become a governor. One of the foremost qualities of 'Umar ibn 'Abd al-'Azīz was his thirst for knowledge. When he was a young child, his father wanted to take him with him from the Levant to Egypt, but he said: 'O father! It may be more beneficial for me if you send me to Madinah to sit with its jurists and learn from their conducts.'[2]

His father agreed to send him to Madinah. He was placed under the supervision of a learned man named Ṣāliḥ ibn Kaysān. During his stay in Madinah, he studied with about thirty-three teachers, eight of whom were Companions of the Prophet while the others were distinguished followers of the Companions (*tābi'ūn*).[3] After years of study, ʿUmar ibn ʿAbd al-ʿAzīz ﷺ stood out, from amongs all his peers for his knowledge, to the extent that he was envied by these peers.

Before his appointment as governor of Madinah, and because of his family background, ʿUmar ibn ʿAbd al-ʿAzīz ﷺ lived a luxurious and relatively passive life. He always left a perfume trail in the streets and alleys where he passed by. After finishing his studies, his uncle and Umayyad caliph, ʿAbd al-Malik ibn Marwān, summoned him to Damascus and married him to his daughter, Fāṭimah bint ʿAbd al-Malik. Fāṭimah was a truly noble woman as her father, four brothers, and uncle were all Umayyad caliphs.

After the death of ʿAbd al-Malik ibn Marwān, his son, al-Walīd ibn ʿAbd al-Malik, was appointed as the new Umayyad caliph. And it was during al-Walīd's reign that ʿUmar ibn ʿAbd al-ʿAzīz ﷺ was appointed governor of Madinah when he was just twenty-four years old.[4] Instead of appointing a council of advisors from his own clan to help him run the affairs of Madinah, he formed a council of jurists, known as the "Ten Jurists of Madinah" (*Majlis Fuqahā' al-Madīnah*)[5] to help him in the discharge of his duties. When he first convened this council, he said:

«إِنِّي دَعَوْتُكُمْ لِأَمْرٍ تُؤْجَرُونَ عَلَيْهِ، وتَكُونُونَ فِيهِ أَعْوانًا عَلى الحَقِّ
ما أُرِيدُ أَنْ أَقْطَعَ أَمْرًا إِلّا بِرَأْيِكُمْ أَوْ بِرَأْيِ مَن حَضَرَ مِنكُمْ، فَإِنْ
رَأَيْتُمْ أَحَدًا يَتَعَدَّى أَوْ بَلَغَكُمْ عَنْ عامِلٍ لِي ظَلامَةً فَأُحَرِّجُ بِاللهِ
عَلى أَحَدٍ بَلَغَهُ ذَلِكَ إِلّا أَبْلَغَنِي. فَجَزَوْهُ خَيْرًا وافْتَرِقُوا».

> I have called you concerning a matter for which you will be rewarded and also enable you to be supporters of the truth. I shall not decide on any matter unless I take your opinion into consideration or the opinions of those present amongst you. If you see anyone transgressing or hear of any injustice committed by one of my officials, I ask you by Allah to inform me about it.[6]

His fame as a just and pious governor spread far and wide to the extent that people began migrating to Madinah from other parts of the Muslim world, that had corrupt and despotic administrators such as al-Ḥajjāj bin Yūsuf in Iraq. As a result, al-Ḥajjāj put pressure on al-Walīd I to remove 'Umar ibn 'Abd al-'Aziz ﷺ from his post, which he did. Unbeknownst to him, though, this setback paved the way for new opportunities for him. Those who are steadfast in their worship and good character traits are always taken care of by Allah ﷻ even if they happen to suffer some hardship for a while. After his dismissal, 'Umar ibn 'Abd al-'Azīz ﷺ moved from the spiritual centre of Islam to its political centre in Damascus where he used his close family ties with the Caliph to continue serving the needs of the Muslim Ummah.

After the death of al-Walīd I, his brother Sulaymān replaced him as caliph. But soon after this, Sulaymān fell ill and he was desperate to find a successor as his sons were too young to succeed him. His advisor, Rajā' ibn Ḥaywah, suggested 'Umar ibn 'Abd al-'Azīz ﷺ as his successor.

Sulaymān accepted the proposal but deputized Ibn Ḥaywah to announce the decision after his death. The announcement was made in a public assembly to everyone's surprise.

"بِسْمِ اللهِ الرَّحْمَنِ الرَّحِيمِ، هَذَا كِتَابٌ مِنْ عَبْدِ اللهِ سُلَيْمَانَ أَمِيرُ الْمُؤْمِنِينَ لِعُمَرَ بْنِ عَبْدِ الْعَزِيزِ، إِنِّي وَلَّيْتُهُ الْخِلَافَةَ مِنْ بَعْدِي، وَمِنْ بَعْدِهِ يَزِيدُ بْنِ عَبْدِ الْمَلِكِ، فَاسْمَعُوا لَهُ وَأَطِيعُوا ".

In the name of Allah, Most Merciful and Most Compassionate. This is a missive from the leader of the believers, Sulaymān to ʿUmar ibn ʿAbd al-ʿAziz. ﷺ I have appointed him as caliph after me, and after him Yazīd ibn ʿAbd al-Malik. So listen to him and obey.[7]

ʿUmar ibn ʿAbd al-ʿAziz ﷺ needed a great deal of convincing to accept this appointment. He recognized the great trust put upon him as caliph and feared the reckoning and judgement of his Lord if he did not do justice to this office or wronged anyone. It was this fear and consciousness of Allah ﷻ that enabled him to do well by the people in his reign which lasted two years and five months.

THE NECESSITY OF REFORM

The word caliph in Arabic, *khalīfah* (خَلِيفَةٌ), means "successor". The Caliph is entrusted with leading the Muslim Ummah. The *Khulafāʾ al-Rāshidūn* were the four successive caliphs who led the Ummah after the death of the Prophet Muhammad ﷺ. They were Abū Bakr al-Ṣiddīq , ʿUmar ibn al-Khaṭṭāb , ʿUthmān ibn ʿAffān , and ʿAlī ibn Abī Ṭālib , respectively. They were responsible for setting an exemplary Islamic political leadership and maintaining a moral and religious ethos in the Muslim polity. Unfortunately, when the Umayyads came to power in 40 AH/661 CE, the post of caliph became overly political and the religious and moral dimensions of the position were somehow neglected.

Some societal ailments from the pre-Islamic era which had been suppressed after the advent of Islam resurfaced when the Umayyad rulers neglected some of the teachings of the Qur'an and Sunnah in the administration of the vast Muslim territory. Racism, tribalism and nepotism became widespread. The Umayyad rulers mishandled the use of the revenues of *bayt al-māl*, the empire's treasury collected from taxes, *zakāt*, and booty, and exploited it for their own lavish lives and enjoyments. Extravagance replaced moral excellence among the ruling class and spirituality was almost absent. This is not to say that the light of Islam had dimmed after the Prophet ﷺ and the reign of the four Rightly-guided caliphs, as there were still masses of scholars and laymen who were firmly following in the footsteps of the early generation of Muslims, including scholars like ʿAlī ibn al-Ḥusayn (also known as Zayn al-ʿĀbidīn), Sālim ibn ʿAbdullāh ibn ʿUmar, and ʿUrwah ibn al-Zubayr. But such eminent personalities, who were symbols of Prophetic behaviour, stayed away from the ruling class. As a result, the might of the Umayyads grew stronger while the scholars' influence on political affairs became insignificant. The leadership of ʿUmar ibn ʿAbd al-ʿAzīz ﵀ was to change this status quo.[8]

قال مَيْمُون بن مِهْرَان: إِنَّ الله يَتَعَاهَدُ النَّاسَ بِنَبِيٍّ بَعْدَ نَبِيٍّ، إِنَّ الله تَعَاهَدَ النَّاسَ بِعُمَرَ بْنِ عَبْدِ الْعَزِيزِ

Maymūn ibn Mihrān said: 'Allah takes care of people through sending prophet after prophet, and verily Allah has taken care of the people through ʿUmar ibn ʿAbd al-ʿAzīz ﵀.'[9]

REFORMATION

As caliph, ʿUmar ibn ʿAbd al-ʿAzīz's ﵀ personal transformation led to the revival of an entire empire. Upon reorganizing the administration of different Muslim territories, his main criteria for selecting governors was the strict adherence to the Book of Allah and the teachings of the Prophet ﷺ as well as competence. He was well aware that his deputies' conducts were reflections of his own conduct and, hence, he felt responsible for their conducts.

ولَـمَّا وُلِّيَ عُمَر بن عَبْـد العَزِيز الـخِلافَـة كَتَبَ إِلَيْـهِ طَاوُسُ: «إِنْ أَرَدْتَ أن يَكونَ عَمُلَكَ خَـيْرًا كُلَّهُ فاسْتَعْمِل أَهْـلَ الـخَيْرِ».

فقال عمر: «كَفَى بِها مَوْعِظَةً».

> When 'Umar Ibn 'Abd al-'Azīz رحمه الله became the caliph, the great Hadith scholar, Ṭāwūs, sent him the following message: 'If you wish all your actions to be good, then you should employ goodly people as your officials.". Upon which 'Umar remarked: "This is quite sufficient as a reminder.'[10]

While previous Umayyad rulers illegally took from the *bayt al-māl* to spend on their own leisurely pursuits, 'Umar ibn 'Abd al-'Azīz رحمه الله was extremely scrupulous about this and cautious not to profit personally from the public treasury. He returned all the jewellery and valuables he received as presents to the *bayt al-māl*. He freed all the slaves owned by the royal household and put an end to all manifestations of extravagance in the royal court. He repealed unjust taxes, standardized weights and measurements in the marketplace and fought corruption among government officials. His financial reforms were so successful that it became hard to find deserving recipients of *zakāt*.[11]

'Umar ibn 'Abd al-'Azīz رحمه الله did not just excel in his administrative duties, he also took it upon himself to promote people's spiritual and religious advancement as a true successor of the Prophet ﷺ, and just as a caliph is supposed to do. Being a scholar in his own right, he sent out countless edicts and letters giving directives to his officials and advising people to return to the ways of the Prophet ﷺ and the Prophetic Companions رضي الله عنهم.

وَكَتَبَ عُمَرُ بن عَبْد العَزِيز إلى بَعْضِ عُمَّالِهِ: «أَمَّا بَعْدُ: فَقَدْ أَمْكَنَتْكَ
القُدْرَةُ مِنَ ظُلْمِ العِبَادِ فَإِذَا هَمَمْتَ بِظُلْمِ أَحَدٍ فَاذْكُرْ قُدْرَةَ اللهِ عَلَيْكَ
واعْلَمْ أَنَّكَ لَا تَأْتِي النَّاسَ شَيْئًا إِلَّا كانَ زَائِلًا عَنْهُمْ بَاقِيًا عَلَيْكَ
واللهُ آخِذٌ لِلمَظْلُومِ مِنَ الظَّالِمِ، والسَّلام».

'Umar ibn 'Abd al-'Azīz ﷺ wrote to one of his
officials, saying: 'Power has placed you in a
position which may allow you to oppress the
servants of Allah. So if you are on the verge of
oppressing anyone, do remember the power
that Allah has over you, and know that you
won't harm people with anything except that
it will pass while the punishment of your
oppression will remain, and Allah will avenge
the oppressed of their oppressors.'[12]

Upon responding to an inquiry made by one of his
governors, al-Jarrāḥ ibn 'Abdullāh, in Central Asia, 'Umar
ibn 'Abd al-'Azīz ﷺ addressed the topic of the state's use
of force against citizens who resist reforms founded on
the Qur'an and Sunnah and his response was clear and
firm. When the governor proposed using 'the sword and
the whip', 'Umar ibn 'Abd al-'Azīz insisted on restraint
and amplifying the state's application of justice and the
truth to placate the citizens.

كَتَبَ عمرُ بن عبد العزيز إلى الجَرَّاح بن عبد الله: «سَلامٌ عَلَيْكَ،
أَمَّا بَعْدُ: كِتَابُكَ يَذْكُرُ أَنَّ أَهْلَ خُرَاسَانَ قَدْ سَاءَتْ رَعِيَّتُهُم، وأَنَّهُ

لا يُصْلِحُهُم إِلَّا السَّيْفُ والسَّوْطُ، وتَسْأَلُنِي أنْ آذَنَ لَكَ، فَقَدْ
كَذَبْتَ؛ بَلْ يُصْلِحُهُم العَدْلُ والحَقُّ، فابْسُطْ ذَلِكَ فِيهِم والسَّلام».

'Peace be upon you, to proceed: I have received your letter in which you mentioned that the people of Khurasan are difficult to govern and that nothing will reform them except the sword and the whip and that you ask my permission in this matter. You have lied, what will reform them is justice and the truth, so spread these two things among them, and peace.'[13]

Perhaps one of 'Umar ibn 'Abd al-'Azīz's greatest accomplishments is his order to officially collect Hadith through scholars such as al-Zuhrī and Mālik ibn Anas.

عن ابْنِ شِهَابٍ قَالَ: «أَمَرَنَا عُمَرُ بن عَبْد العَزِيزِ بِجَمْعِ السُّنَنِ،
فَكَتَبْنَاها دَفْتَرًا دَفْتَرًا، فَبَعَثَ إلى كُلِّ أَرْضٍ لَهُ عَلَيْهَا سُلْطَانٌ دَفْتَرًا».

Al-Zuhrī relates that 'Umar ibn 'Abd al-'Azīz commanded us to gather all the sound narrations. So we collected them in ledgers which were then sent to all the lands upon which he had authority.[14]

He upheld the *Sharī'ah* and put an emphasis on *da'wah,* i.e. spreading the message of Islam to non-Muslims, just as the Prophet ﷺ did.

قَالَ الإِمَامُ أَحْمَد بن حَنْبَل: «لَا أَدْرِي قَوْلَ أَحَدٍ مِنَ التَّابِعِينَ حُجَّةً إِلَّا قَوْلَ عُمَرَ بْن عَبْدِ العَزِيزِ».

Imam Aḥmad ibn Ḥanbal said: 'I don't know of any of the followers of the Companions (*tābiʿīn*) whose legal opinion is a conclusive legal proof except ʿUmar ibn ʿAbd al-ʿAzīz.'[15]

HIS CHARACTER TRAITS

Cheating, lying, and drinking were commonplace in the lands of the Caliphate before the appointment of ʿUmar ibn ʿAbd al- ʿAzīz ﵀ as caliph. Before his reign, rulers were in the habit of usurping people's wealth or even killing them for the flimsiest of reasons. ʿUmar ibn ʿAbd al-ʿAzīz ﵀ changed all that. His sacrifices, strong *īmān* and resolve allowed him to make a difference.

Oftentimes, people's ambitions are motivated by a political prism which hinders their ability for introspection and self-growth and limits their effect on those around them. There are also those who behave in exactly the opposite way by being so self-absorbed in their spirituality that they ignore the suffering and problems of others. Both these extremes yield limited results. The Prophetic Companions learnt from the Prophet ﷺ, particularly as outlined in Surahs *al-Muzzammil* and *al-Muddaththir*, that in order to change society, there must be a balance between personal growth, and self-purification, social reform and change. ʿUmar ibn ʿAbd al-ʿAzīz was one of those who achieved the rare feat of striking such a balance. His sacrifice and generosity impacted all those around him, especially his family. Before his appointment as caliph, he was extremely generous by distributing all the gifts he received from his father. But upon becoming a caliph, not only did he give up all of his own wealth, but he also asked his wife to do the same, even though she was fully entitled to keep her own wealth and possessions. According to Ibn Kathīr 🕮, no woman was given as much gold as Fāṭimah on the day of her marriage. However, being a strong and pious woman who believed in her husband and in what he wanted to achieve, she wholeheartedly proclaimed that she would choose him over mountains of gold. Indeed, this came as no surprise as both of them were true embodiments of the verse:

وَمِنَ ٱلنَّاسِ مَنْ يَشْرِي نَفْسَهُ ٱبْتِغَآءَ مَرْضَاتِ اللهِ

But other men there are that sell themselves desiring Allah's good pleasure.[16]

They were the kind of individuals who would rather renounce all the wealth and luxuries of the world in order to see the Prophet ﷺ smiling back at them on the Day of Judgment.

It is narrated that once, upon the approach of Eid, 'Umar ibn 'Abd al-'Azīz's wife requested him to take one-month's advance salary to buy new clothes for his children. They had been wearing the same tattered clothes for some time and she did not want them to be embarrassed in front of their relatives. ʿUmar ibn ʿAbd al-ʿAzīz ﷺ went to his treasurer, Muzāḥim, and asked him for a month's salary in advance, but his treasurer responded, 'O Leader of the Believers! Can you guarantee that you will live for another month to repay this amount of money?'

Taken aback, ʿUmar ibn ʿAbd al-ʿAzīz ﷺ said that he could give no such guarantee. On Eid day, relatives, officials, and others came to visit ʿUmar ibn ʿAbd al-ʿAzīz and were greeted by his children who were wearing the same old clothes. Later that day, ʿUmar ibn ʿAbd al-ʿAzīz ﷺ was in tears when he met his children and apologized to them for not being able to provide for them. But his eldest child, ʿAbd al-Malik, responded: 'O father, don't apologize. Today was one of the happiest days of our lives. Never have we been able to hold our heads up higher than today. Today, we let the world know that our father, the Leader of the believers, would never take even one dirham which is not rightfully his. Our father provides for us only that which is lawful and permissible.'[17]

Today, it is hard to imagine someone who rules over all the Muslim lands living such an austere and contended life. He did not even have enough money to go for *Ḥajj*. He was sometimes late for the Friday prayer because he had to wait for his washed shirt to dry as he did not have another one to wear. He was also careful not to use the privileges offered by the state for his own private affairs. When he discussed state affairs, he lighted the candles provided by the state, otherwise he lighted his own candles.[18]

حَدَّثَنَا عَمْرُو بنُ مُهَاجِرٍ:أَنَّ عُمَرَ بنَ عَبْدِ العَزِيزِ كَانَ تُسْرَجُ عَلَيْهِ
الشَّمْعَةُ مَا كَانَ فِي حَوَائِجِ الـمُسْلِمِيْنَ، فَإِذَا فَرَغَ، أَطْفَأَهَا،
وَأَسْرَجَ عَلَيْهِ سِرَاجَهُ.

'Amr ibn Muhājir said: 'A candle was lit for
'Umar ibn 'Abd al-'Azīz for as long as he was
dealing with the affairs of the people. When
he finished dealing with those affairs, he
put out that candle and lighted his own,
private candle.'

'Umar ibn 'Abd al-'Azīz's wife also testified that
he spent the night standing in prayer and crying in his
supplications to Allah , when most people were resting
or spending time with their spouses. During his reign,
non-Muslims converted to Islam in record numbers as a
result of his just rule and reforms. 'Umar ibn 'Abd al-
'Azīz summed up well about the force that was driving
him in life when he said:

«أَيُّهَا النَّاسُ، إِنَّ لِي نَفْسًا تَوَّاقَةً لَا تُعْطَى شَيْئًا إِلَّا تَاقَتْ إِلَى مَا هُوَ
أَعْلَى مِنْهُ، وَإِنِّي لَـمَّا أَعْطِيتُ الخِلَافَةَ تَاقَتْ نَفْسِي إِلَى مَا هُوَ أَعْلَى مِنْهَا
وَهِيَ الجَنَّةُ، فَأَعِينُونِي عَلَيْهَا يَرْحَمْكُمُ اللهُ».

'O people! I have an insatiable and ambitious
soul; whenever I get something, I long for
something higher than it. And now that I have
been given the caliphate, my soul is longing

for what is higher than it, which is Paradise, so please help me to achieve it, may Allah have mercy on you.'[19]

In his youth, he possessed all the worldly possession anyone could hope for in his time . As Caliph, he gave up the *Dunyā* altogether and set his sight on *Jannah* and this dictated his words and actions. When some people advised him to live like the king that he was, he recited to them:

قُلْ إِنِّي أَخَافُ إِنْ عَصَيتُ رَبِّي عَذَابَ يَوْمٍ عَظِيمٍ

Say: 'Indeed I fear, if I should rebel against my Lord, the chastisement of a dreadful day.'[20]

HIS DEATH

There has to be opponents and enemies to any individual who follows the path of righteousness, justice and piety. When 'Umar ibn 'Abd al-'Azīz ﷺ chose to follow the Prophetic way and apply justice and the truth in his reign, he thwarted the agendas and ulterior motives of many people around him in the royal court. Many among the wealthy and the powerful, especially from within the Umayyad clan, personally benefited from the rule of previous Umayyad rulers due to their family ties. 'Umar ibn 'Abd al-'Azīz ﷺ had undone numerous institutionalised injustices and restored the rights of those who were unlawfully denied them.

Scheming amongst the Umayyad clan and the tense relation they had with 'Umar ibn 'Abd al-'Azīz ﷺ were no secret. He was even advised to have someone check his food for poison and guard him while he prayed. To this he replied:

«لَوْ جَعَلْتَ عَلَى طَعَامِكَ أَمِينًا لَا تُغْتَالَ، وَحَرَسًا إِذَا صَلَّيْتَ لَا تُغْتَالَ، وَتَنَحَّ عَنِ الطَّاعُونِ». فَقَالَ: «اللَّهُمَّ إِنْ كُنْتَ تَعْلَمُ أَنِّي أَخَافُ يَوْمًا دُونَ يَوْمِ القِيَامَةِ فَلَا تُؤَمِّنْ خَوْفِي».

'O Allah , if you know that I fear any day other than the Day of Judgment, then do not make me safe from that fear.'[21]

There is difference of opinion regarding how 'Umar ibn 'Abd al-'Azīz ﷺ passed away. Some historians are of the opinion that he died a natural death, but there are those who maintain that some powerful people within the Umayyad clan plotted against him and bribed one of his workers to poison him. 'Umar ibn 'Abd al-'Azīz ﷺ was sick for twenty days in which his pain gradually increased until he finally returned to his Lord in the year 101 AH/720 CE.

Before his death, many people suggested that he travel to Madinah so that he may be buried next to the Prophet ﷺ and the two Khulafa after him. Upon hearing this, he said:

«وَاللهِ لَأَنْ يُعَذِّبَنِّي اللهُ بِكُلِّ عَذَابٍ إِلَّا النَّارَ، فَإِنَّهُ لَا صَبْرَ لِي عَلَيْهَا، أَحَبُّ إِلَيَّ مِنْ أَنْ يَعْلَمَ اللهُ مِنْ قَلْبِي أَنِّي لِذَلِكَ الْـمَوْضِعِ أَهْلٌ».

'By Allah! If Allah were to chastise me with every possible chastisement apart from that of hellfire, for I cannot withstand that, is more beloved to me than Allah knowing that I think that I deserve to be buried in that place.'[22]

'Ubayd Ibn Hasān reported some of the glad tidings that 'Umar ibn 'Abd al-'Azīz ﷺ received shortly before his death, saying:

«لـمَّا احْتَضَرَ عُمَرُ بْنُ عَبْدِ الْعَزِيزِ قَالَ: اخْرُجُوا عَنِّي، فَقَعَدَ مَسْلَمَةُ وَفَاطِمَةُ عَلَى الْبَابِ فَسَمِعُوهُ يَقُولُ: مَرْحَبًا بِهَذِهِ الوُجُوهِ، لَيْسَتْ بِوُجُوهِ إِنْسٍ وَلَا جَانٍّ. قال: ثُمَّ قَالَ: «تِلْكَ الدَّارُ الْآخِرَةُ نَجْعَلُهَا لِلَّذِينَ لَا يُرِيدُونَ عُلُوًّا فِي الْأَرْضِ وَلَا فَسَادًا وَالْعَاقِبَةُ لِلْمُتَّقِينَ». قَالَ: ثُمَّ هَدَأَ الصَّوْتُ. فَقَالَ مَسْلَمَةُ لِفَاطِمَةَ: قَدْ قُبِضَ صَاحِبُكِ. فَدَخَلُوا فَوَجَدُوهُ قَدْ قُبِضَ وَغُمِّضَ وَسُوِّيَ».

When 'Umar was near death he told those around him : 'Go out of the room, so they did and Maslamah [ibn 'Abd al-Malik] and Fāṭimah sat outside the door, upon which they heard him say: "Welcome to these faces, which are neither faces of humans nor jinn." Then he began reciting the verse: *That is the Last Abode;*

We appoint it for those who desire not exorbitance in the earth, nor corruption. The issue ultimate is to the godfearing. Then he fell silent, upon which Maslamah said to Fāṭimah: "Your husband is dead" and on entering the room, they found him dead, having had his eyes closed and his body straightened.'[23]

CONCLUSION

One may not be a leader of a nation or men, but one can lead with excellence and justice in mind upon fulfilling any duty or responsibility one is entrusted with. Everyone can aspire to the example set by ʿUmar ibn ʿAbd al-ʿAzīz through imbibing the qualities of sacrifice, integrity, and understanding. The Prophet ﷺ taught us that whoever loves this *dunyā* excessively will harm his *ākhirah*, and whoever loves his *ākhirah* may lose in this *dunyā*. However, the Prophet ﷺ enjoined the believers to prefer that which is imperishable and everlasting.

عَنْ أَبِي مُوسَى الأَشْعَرِي رَضِيَ اللهُ عَنْهُ أَنَّ رَسُولَ اللهِ ﷺ قَالَ :
«مَنْ أَحَبَّ دُنْيَاهُ أَضَرَّ بِآخِرَتِهِ وَمَنْ أَحَبَّ آخِرَتَهُ أَضَرَّ بِدُنْيَاهُ، فَآثِرُوا
مَا يَبْقَى عَلَى مَا يَفْنَى»[24]

Abū Mūsā al-Ashʿarī narrated that the Prophet ﷺ said: 'Whosoever loves his *Dunyā* harms his *Ākhirah*, and whosoever loves his *Ākhirah* harms his *Dunyā*. So give preference to that which lasts over that which perishes.'

With the *ākhirah* in mind, one can enact change within oneself as well as within those around oneself.

الحسن البصري

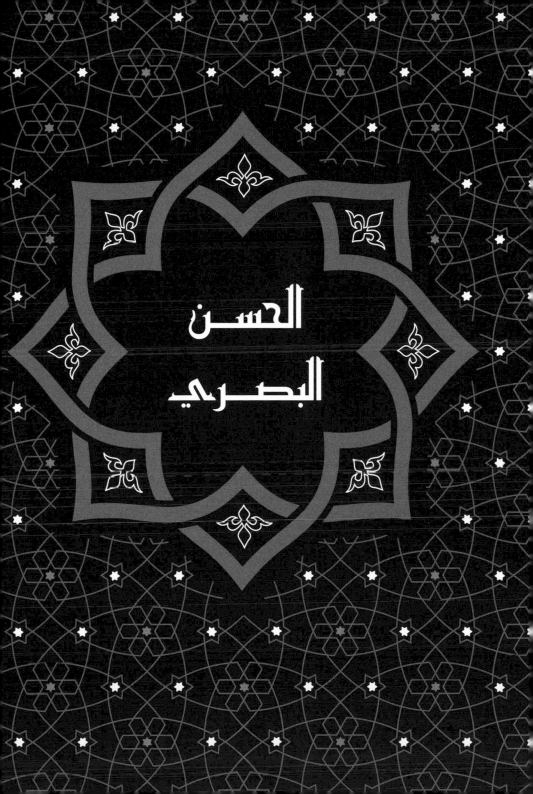

Al-Ḥasan al-Baṣrī

The Pinnacle of Piety and Eloquence

INTRODUCTION

AL-ḤASAN AL-BAṢRĪ ﵀ was a follower of the Prophetic Companions (*tābiʿī*). His study with a number of Prophetic Companions, from a tender age, helped him to become a scholar of the highest calibre. As someone blessed with keen insight, he was troubled by the hypocrisy of the Umayyad ruling elite. Through his impassioned speech and incredible spiritual prowess, he fought against hypocrisy which was then widespread in Basra and called for a return to the straight path of Islam.

Following the death of ʿUmar ibn ʿAbd al-ʿAzīz, ﵀ the Umayyad ruling elite began reshaping the policies of the their empire, taking into account their ulterior motives and personal interests, just as they did before the reign of ʿUmar ibn ʿAbd al-ʿAzīz. ﵀ Although there was a semblance of Islamic conduct within the governing elite, they were in many aspects far from true adherence to the *Dīn*. Unlike the generation of the Prophetic Companions who imbibed the teachings of the *Dīn*, the Umayyad ruling elite used religion as a facade which allowed them to abuse their power in its name. Excessive indulgence in power struggle, politics and wealth brought back to the fore the same illicit practices prevalent before the advent of Islam. In such scenarios, divine intervention is needed to refocus society on the obedience of Allah and the noble practices of the Prophet ﷺ. Al-Ḥasan al-Baṣrī ﷺ was one of the tools of divine intervention that brought about a change in the Muslim society.

EARLY YEARS

Al-Ḥasan al-Baṣrī ﷺ was born in the year 21 AH/642 CE. His father, Yasār, was a servant of Zayd ibn Thābit ﷺ, one of the scribes of the Prophet ﷺ who is primarily remembered as one of the Prophetic Companions who gathered the different parchments upon which the verses of the whole Qur'an were written into one single copy, i.e. the *Muṣḥaf* that is known today. His mother, Khayrah, was a maid in the home of Umm Salamah ﷺ, one of the wives of the Prophet ﷺ. Al-Ḥasan al-Baṣrī ﷺ grew up in the holy city of Madinah where he witnessed the practice of Islam in its most authentic and pristine form Umm Salamah ﷺ, Zayd ibn Thābit ﷺ and other Companions of the Prophet ﷺ. As a child, he was taken to 'Umar ibn al-Khaṭṭāb ﷺ, who reigned for another two years after the birth of al-Ḥasan al-Baṣrī, ❀ he named him al-Ḥasan, and then he made the following *du'ā'* for him:

اللَّهُمَّ فَقِّهْهُ فِي الدِّينِ وَحَبِّبْهُ إِلَى النَّاسِ

O Allah! Grant him true understanding of the
Dīn and make him beloved to the people[25]

When al-Ḥasan al-Baṣrī ❀ was asked about the determining factor that shaped his outlook on life, he said:

سَنَتَانِ مِنْ خِلَافَةِ عُمَرَ

It was the two years of the reign of 'Umar.[26]

Al-Ḥasan al-Baṣrī's ❀ early company with a number of Prophetic Companions highlights the importance of keeping good company in a world replete with challenges and temptations. He was fortunate to learn from the wisdom of Zayd ibn Thabit ❀, Umm Salamah ❀ and other Companions of the Prophet ❀. His experience also stresses the importance of learning from living scholars for, even though learning from books has its own merit and benefits, it remains insufficient according to all genuine scholars of sacred knowledge. This is because a student of sacred knowledge must not just learn or memorise new things but he must also interiorize the spiritual states and piety of his teachers. The lesson here is the necessity of seeking the company of those who are knowledgeable and righteous. In order to become better people, Islam emphasizes the importance of *ṣuḥbah* (companionship). *Ṣuḥbah* and the wisdom that one acquires from it distinguishes knowledge from mere information. Good character and healthy lifestyle choices can be acquired and developed if one has a good circle of friends and mentors.

عَنِ ابْنِ عَبَّاسٍ، قَالَ: «قِيلَ : يَا رَسُولَ اللهِ! أَيُّ جُلَسَائِنَا خَيْرٌ؟»
قَالَ: «مَنْ ذَكَّرَكُمْ بِاللهِ رُؤْيَتُهُ، وَزَادَ فِي عِلْمِكُمْ مَنْطِقُهُ،
وَذَكَّرَكُمْ بِالآخِرَةِ عَمَلُهُ».

Ibn ʿAbbās reported that it was said:
'O Messenger of Allah! Who is the best
among those with whom we keep company?'
So he replied: 'It is those whose mere seeing
reminds you of Allah and whose speech
increases your knowledge and whose actions
remind you of the Afterlife.'[27]

The Prophet ﷺ taught his Companions, trained and guided them to developing perfect character traits. These noble Companions were wary of complacency and strove to teach the generation after them what they had learnt from the Prophet ﷺ. Each person is innately good and possesses great potential, but it is only through surrounding oneself with people who appreciate such goodness and potential that one can achieve personal and communal change

Al-Ḥasan al-Baṣrī's ﵀ character was moulded by some Prophetic Companions who were his teachers and role models. It is, therefore, no surprise that, despite having never met the Prophet ﷺ, he exemplified the Prophetic teachings and character traits.

سَمِعْتُ أبا بُرْدَةَ يَقُولُ: «ما رَأَيْتُ رَجُلًا قَطُّ لَمْ يَصْحَبِ النَّبِيَّ ﷺ أَشْبَهَ بِأَصْحابِ رَسُولِ اللهِ ﷺ مِن هَذا الشَّيْخِ، يَعْنِي الحَسَنَ».

I heard Abū Burdah say: 'I have never met a man who was not a Companion of the Prophet ﷺ but who most resembled the Companions of the Prophet ﷺ like this venerable man (meaning al-Ḥasan al-Baṣrī).'[28]

BASRA

Al-Ḥasan al-Baṣrī and his family moved to Basra, Iraq, in approximately 36 AH/656 CE. This city was built by ʿUmar ibn al-Khaṭṭāb in 16 AH/636 CE as a garrison settlement on the border of the Sassanid Empire. It grew into a major financial and political hub during the Umayyad period, eventually becoming the scene of shady business dealings and corrupt leadership. While this deviancy from true Islamic teachings was addressed during the reign of ʿUmar ibn ʿAbd al-ʿAzīz, some Umayyad rulers turned a blind eye to a great deal of activities and behaviours that clashed with the Islamic teachings. Being a native of Madinah and a student of Prophetic Companions, al-Ḥasan al-Baṣrī was shocked at what he witnessed in Basra. He therefore embarked on a social campaign to instil a sense of morality and spiritual awareness in the public sphere. His indefatigable efforts and reforming zeal caused a massive cultural shift and stirred moral uplifting in this city which have been keenly reported and highly praised in Islamic literature. In particular, his masterful oratory skills was said to surpass those of any scholar or preacher in the Hejaz or the Levant.

حَدَّثنا زَكَرِيّا، قالَ: سَمِعْتُ الحَسَنَ يَقُولُ: «إنَّ الإِيمَانَ لَيْسَ بِالتَّحَلِّي
وَلَا بِالتَّمَنِّي، إِنَّمَا الإِيمَانُ مَا وقَرَ فِي القَلْبِ وصَدَّقَهُ العَمَلُ».

Zakariyā reported that he heard al-Ḥasan
al-Baṣrī say: 'Verily, faith (*īmān*) is not through
appropriation of character traits nor through
mere wishful thinking; it is rather what is
deeply imbedded in the heart and
confirmed by actions.'[29]

What was it that distinguished al-Ḥasan al-Baṣrī ﵀ from many scholars of his time and bequeath that tremendous ability to change hearts? First, he took the guidance he received from his teachers to heart and remained grounded as exhorted by his eminent mentors. Second, he was an embodiment of asceticism, sacrificing the paltry pleasures of this world for the good pleasure of God. His distrust of political power and shunning of wealth protected him from any attempts to bribe him, which empowered him and made him a role model in Basra. His exemplary lifestyle, immense knowledge, and unwavering practice of the *Dīn* awakened people's hearts.

Hearts corrupted by sinning are discontent in this world and shall face a detrimental consequence in the Hereafter.

عَنْ أَبِي هُرَيْرَةَ، قَالَ: قَالَ رَسُولُ اللهِ ﷺ : إذَا أذنَبَ العَبْدُ نُكِتَ فِي قَلْبِهِ نُكْتَةٌ سَوْدَاءُ، فإنْ تابَ صُقِلَ مِنْها، فإنْ عادَ عادَتْ حتى تَعْظُمَ فِي قَلْبِهِ، فذلكَ الرَّانُ الَّذي قالَ اللهُ: « كَلاَّ بَلْ رَانَ عَلَى قُلُوبِهِمْ مَا كَانُوا يَكْسِبُونَ ».

Abū Hurayrah reported that the Messenger of Allah ﷺ said: 'When the servant commits a sin, a black spot is dotted on his heart. If he repents, the heart will be polished [and the spot is removed]. But if he goes back to the sin, it (i.e. the black spot) returns so much so that it is magnified in his heart. That is the *rān* about which Allah says: (*No indeed; but that they were earning has rusted upon their hearts*).'[30]

A pure heart cleansed through forgiveness is drawn nearer to Allah ﷻ and His Messenger Muhammad ﷺ. The person who possesses such a heart reflects the light of Islam.

قَالَ عَبْدُ اللهِ بْنُ عَبّاسٍ رَضِيَ اللهُ عَنْهُمَا: «إنَّ لِلْحَسَنَةِ ضِيَاءً فِي الوَجْهِ ونُورًا فِي القَلْبِ وسَعَةً فِي الرِّزْقِ وقُوَّةً فِي البَدَنِ ومَحَبَّةً فِي

قُلُوبِ الخَلْقِ، وإِنَّ لِلسَّيِّئَةِ سَوادًا فِي الوَجْهِ وظُلْمَةً فِي القَلْبِ ووَهَنًا فِي البَدَنِ ونَقْصًا فِي الرِّزْقِ وبِغْضَةً فِي قُلُوبِ الخَلْقِ».

Ibn ʿAbbās 🌸 said: 'A good deed leaves a radiance in the face, a light in the heart, and causes the expansion of sustenance, strength of the body, and love in the hearts of created beings. A sin, on the other hand, leaves darkness on the face, estrangement in the heart, weakness in the body, and causes a decrease in sustenance and detestation in the hearts of created beings.'[31]

HIS QUALITIES

Al-Ḥasan al-Baṣrī 🌸 was endowed with a number of beautiful character traits from his early childhood which he maintained throughout his life. Foremost among these is his commitment to sacred knowledge, his willingness to denounce immorality and speak against corruption, his asceticism, and his natural connection with all peoples.

From Madinah to Basra, it was a priority for al-Ḥasan al-Baṣrī 🌸 to gain proficiency in all aspects of the religion of Islam.

عَنِ الرَّبِيعِ بْنِ أَنَسٍ قَالَ: «اخْتَلَفْتُ إِلَى الحَسَنِ عَشْرَ سِنِينَ، أَوْ مَا شَاءَ اللهُ مِنْ ذَلِكَ، فَلَيْسَ مِنْ يَوْمٍ إِلَّا أَسْمَعُ مِنْهُ مَا لَمْ أَسْمَعْ قَبْلَ ذَلِكَ».

Al-Rabīʿ ibn Anas said: 'I frequented al-Ḥasan al-Baṣrī 🌸 about ten years or so and every day

I heard from him something new which I did
not hear before.'[32]

Today, some people, especially in the West, speak as if they were scholars of the highest calibre but without having gone through a fraction of the hardship that our righteous predecessors had suffered in their quest for sacred knowledge, neither having spent the long years necessary for attaining the highest standard of scholarship required in Islam. We should not speak of imbibing the states of one's unworldly and Godfearing teachers and avoiding any scholars who does not practise what he teaches. Accumulating the necessary analytical skills and understanding of authentic sources and teachers are vital. Hence, teaching and preaching from those who do not possess the appropriate scholarly and moral qualifications can cause irreparable damage to individuals and society, and even lead to questioning the integrity of the Islamic teachings. However, even those who are well grounded and have a strong understanding of Islam's teachings may struggle to impart them to others. One should learn to teach others for there is a tremendous honour and privilege in transmitting the teachings of the Prophet ﷺ. And there is no harm if one cannot do so, as there are many paths to Allah. But if one is on the path of teaching others, then one must focus on improving the ways one imparts knowledge to others and be a good example to those around him.

Al-Ḥasan al-Baṣrī combined both characteristics: he surpassed all the scholars of his time in knowledge and was loved by the people.

Second, al-Ḥasan al-Baṣrī was on a mission to expose Basra's wayward practices and invited people back to the pure teachings of the Prophet ﷺ. Just as the Prophet ﷺ waged a campaign to eradicate all non-Islamic practices in Arabia, al-Ḥasan al-Baṣrī ﵀ identified issues in Basra, such as fraud and oppression committed by the ruling elite and widespread hypocrisy and strove to eradicate them.[33]

وَلَقَدْ كَانَ الحَسَنُ البَصْرِي رَحِمَهُ اللهُ أَشْبَهَ النَّاسِ كَلاماً بِكَلامِ
الأَنْبِيَاءِ عَلَيْهِمِ الصَّلاةُ والسَّلامُ وَأَقْرَبَهُمْ هَدْياً مِنَ الصَّحَابَةِ ﵃.

'Al-Ḥasan al-Baṣrī ﵀ was the closest in speech to the speech of the Prophets, peace and blessings be upon him, just as he was the closest in demeanour to the demeanour of the Prophetic Companions ﵃.'[34]

From the pulpit, he reminded his listeners about the dire consequences of committing fraud, swindling, corruption and oppression. He exhorted them to follow the teachings of Islam and reminded them that wealth and power mean very little in the *Ākhirah* unless they are used as a mean to please Allah ﷻ.

وَقَالَ الْحَسَنُ: «بِئْسَ الرَّفِيقَانِ: الدِّينَارُ وَالدِّرْهَمُ،
لَا يَنْفَعَانِكَ حَتَّى يُرَافِقَانِكَ».

Al-Ḥasan al-Baṣrī ﵀ said: 'The two worse companions are gold pieces (*al-dīnār*) and silver pieces (*al-dirham*); they cannot benefit you unless they accompany you [through being used for the sake of Allah].'[35]

While possession of money tends to pull a lot of people away from their *Dīn*, we should not be contemptible towards those who possess wealth. Wealth and poverty are usually neutral states, as both can be either a blessing or a punishment. What is important in the matter is whether they make one a better or a worse Muslim and person.

Al-Ḥasan al-Baṣrī's condemnation of societal injustices was so loud and eloquent that it was difficult for those present not to be swayed by his sermons. Those who attended his gatherings were moved to their bones and hastened to change their lives. Popularity and fame usually harm one's relationship with Allah. However, the individuals who are enslaved by the material pleasures of this materialistic world neglect their relationship with Allah, and eventually forget that this world is fleeting and temporary. Al-Ḥasan al-Baṣrī strove to remind people that they will face the Day of Judgment and an eternity of either bliss or damnation will be decreed for them according to their attitudes and actions in this world.

قَالَ الْحَسَنُ: «ابْنَ آدَمَ! إِنَّمَا أَنْتَ أَيَّامٌ كُلَّمَا ذَهَبَ يَوْمٌ ذَهَبَ بَعْضُكَ».

Al-Ḥasan al-Baṣrī said: 'O son of Adam! You are but a few days, whenever a day elapses, a part of you also elapses too.'[36]

وَقَالَ الْحَسَنُ: «فَضَحَ الْـمَوْتُ الدُّنْيَا فَلَمْ يَتْرُكْ فِيهَا لِذِي لُبٍّ فَرَحًا».

Al-Ḥasan al-Baṣrī ﵀ said: 'Death has exposed this worldly life: it has left no joy for anyone who has a sound intellect."[37]

Chasing the material pleasures and gains of this world is a futile endeavour. One always desires more and one's appetite for the material world eventually becomes insatiable. Those who love Allah, like al-Ḥasan al-Baṣrī ﵀ and other pious predecessors, make concerted efforts to resist the illusions of this *Dunyā*. They trained their egos, or lower selves, to comply with all the commandments of Allah.

عَنِ الْحَسَنِ أَنَّهُ كَانَ يَقُولُ: «مَنْ أَحَبَّ الدُّنْيَا وَسَرَّتْهُ ذَهَبَ خَوْفُ الْآخِرَةِ مِنْ قَلْبِهِ، وَمَا مِنْ عَبْدٍ يَزْدَادُ عِلْمًا وَيَزْدَادُ عَلَى الدُّنْيَا حِرْصًا، إِلَّا ازْدَادَ إِلَى اللهِ عَزَّ وَجَلَّ بُغْضًا وَازْدَادَ مِنَ اللهِ بُعْدًا»

It is reported that al-Haṣan al-Baṣrī ﵀ said: 'Whoever loves this world and is pleased with it makes the fear of the Hereafter depart from his heart; and there is no servant who increases in knowledge and yet increases, at the same time, in greed for this world except Allah's detestation for him increases and his distance from Allah widens.'[38]

Lastly, his sincerity in bettering people's spiritual condition and his goodwill towards Allah's created beings cemented his legacy in the community. One day, while sitting with a group of students, a man came and complained about his depleted finances and asked for al-Ḥasan al-Baṣrī's advice. The latter responded by saying: 'Seek Allah's forgiveness'. Later, in the same gathering, another individual complained to al-Ḥasan al-Baṣrī ﵀ about not being able to have children. The Imam gave the same advice he gave to the man mentioned above, saying: 'Seek Allah's forgiveness.' Lastly, a farmer came to him to complain about his poor harvest and asked al-Ḥasan al-Baṣrī ﵀ to pray for him. Surprisingly, his advice to the farmer was also the same: 'Seek Allah's forgiveness.' His students asked him about why he gave the same advice for three different situations. Al-Ḥasan al-Baṣrī simply pointed out that the advice was not his but rather Allah's for He, the Most High says in the Qur'an:

فَقُلْتُ اسْتَغْفِرُوا رَبَّكُمْ إِنَّهُ كَانَ غَفَّارًا يُرْسِلِ السَّمَاءَ عَلَيْكُم مِّدْرَارًا
وَيُمْدِدْكُم بِأَمْوَالٍ وَبَنِينَ وَيَجْعَل لَّكُمْ جَنَّاتٍ وَيَجْعَل لَّكُمْ أَنْهَارًا [39]

… and I said, "Ask you forgiveness of your Lord; surely He is ever All-forgiving, and He will loose heaven upon you in torrents and will succour you with wealth and sons, and will appoint for you gardens, and will appoint for you rivers…"

Indeed, sometimes one tries to construct convoluted solutions to situations that have already been addressed in the Islamic tradition in a straightforward manner. One can learn a great deal from the example of al-Ḥasan al-Baṣrī ﵀

for, despite his vast knowledge and rhetorical eloquence, he often referred to the Qur'an instead of venturing his personal views and explanations. Reference to the Qur'an and Hadith greatly resonates with all people regardless of their political bias or level of learning because all people hold these two sources as authentic and undisputed.

HIS DEATH

Al-Ḥasan al-Baṣrī passed away at the age of 86 in 107 AH/728 CE after having instituted enormous change in the behaviour of people in the city of Basra. Thanks to his efforts, a considerable number of people from among the elite class reformed their ways and the *Dīn* was revived. All of Basra showed up to al-Ḥasan al-Baṣrī's r *janāzah*, so much so that the central mosque of Basra was completely empty at the ʿAṣr prayer of that same day.[40] The life and career of al-Ḥasan al-Baṣrī teach us numerous lessons, such as how keeping excellent company forms great individuals, how self-discipline is key in remaining true to Allah and why knowledge is a prerequisite to calling people to Islam.

The life of al-Ḥasan al-Baṣrī is a testament to how to attain guidance and become people of the straight path who are grounded in knowledge and are effectively able to bring people to Islam. His life inspires one to look for better company and godly teachers who can take one by the hand when one stumbles and equips one to do the same with others.

إمام ابو حنيفة

Imam Abū Ḥanīfa

The Treasure store of Jurisprudence

INTRODUCTION

THE PROPHET ﷺ was once sitting with his Companions when he put his arm around Salmān al-Fārisī ؓ and said: 'If perfected faith were to be found in the Pleiades, men from among these [pointing to Salmān] would acquire it.'

كُنَّا جُلُوسًا عِنْدَ النَّبِيِّ ﷺ إِذْ نَزَلَتْ عَلَيْهِ سُورَةُ الْجُمُعَةِ فَلَمَّا قَرَأَ «وَآخَرِينَ مِنْهُمْ لَـمَّا يَلْحَقُوا بِهِمْ» قَالَ رَجُلٌ: مَنْ هَؤُلَاءِ يَا رَسُولَ اللهِ فَلَمْ يُرَاجِعْهُ النَّبِيُّ ﷺ حَتَّى سَأَلَهُ مَرَّةً أَوْ مَرَّتَيْنِ أَوْ ثَلَاثًا - قَالَ - وَفِينَا سَلْمَانُ الْفَارِسِيُّ - قَالَ - فَوَضَعَ النَّبِيُّ ﷺ يَدَهُ عَلَى سَلْمَانَ ثُمَّ قَالَ: «لَوْ كَانَ الإِيمَانُ عِنْدَ الثُّرَيَّا لَنَالَهُ رِجَالٌ مِنْ هَؤُلَاءِ».

In this hadith, the Prophet ﷺ predicted that a great *mujaddid*, reviver of Islam, will come from

Persia. Many interpreted this hadith as referring to Imam Abū Ḥanīfah ﵀.[41]

Al-Nuʿmān ibn Thābit, more commonly known as Imam Abū Ḥanīfah ﵀, was the first of the four codifiers and standard-setters of the Islamic schools of jurisprudence (*fiqh*) that stood the test of time and have been accepted by consensus of *Ahl al-Sunnah wa'l-Jamāʿah* (Sunni Orthodoxy). He is nicknamed *al-Imām al-Aʿẓam*, The Greatest Imam. The continued adherence to his legal framework and the sheer number of the adherents to his juristic school is a testament to the strength and comprehensiveness of his legal legacy.

EARLY LIFE

Imam Abū Ḥanīfah's ﵀ parents were known in their community as God-conscious and upright Muslims. The story goes that the two met when Thābit, Imam Abū Ḥanīfah's father, ate a piece of fruit that had fallen from someone's garden. Fearful that he ate something belonging to someone else without permission, he approached the owner of the garden to make amend for what he had done. Impressed by Thābit's piety and godfearingness, the owner wanted to test him and told him that the only way to make amend was to marry his daughter who was severely disabled, being blind, deaf and dumb. As much as he was distraught and bewildered by this turn of events, he thought he had no choice but to make amends for his wrongdoing and marry the owner's daughter. However, after the marriage was done, and to his surprise, he found out that not only the young woman he married was remarkably beautiful, but she was also not blind, deaf or dumb. This young woman went on to explain to him that she was deaf to what displeases Allah, dumb because she never utters what angers Allah and she was blind from what is forbidden to look at. Abū Ḥanīfah ﵀ was born to these two pious and godfearing parents in the city of Kufa in the year 80 AH/689 CE.

Imam Abū Ḥanīfah ﵀ was tall and dark skinned. From the age of five, he began helping his father in his textile trade which allowed him to learn the trade as he grew older and later becomes financially independent because of it. Throughout his life, he acted and presented himself as an affluent and wealthy man. He achieved success in his business while upholding Islamic business ethics which include shunning usury, not taking Allah's name in vain by swearing to promote one's product, not hiking the prices of commodities unnecessarily, not taking advantage of poor customers and abstention from selling defective products. It is worth mentioning that Abū Ḥanīfah ﵀ practised these Islamic qualities in trade before he began taking interest in pursuing the Islamic sciences. This demonstrates that he was God-conscious and that Allah was his sole motivation. Imam Abū Ḥanīfah ﵀ was also gracious to the poor judging from the amount of *ṣadaqah* he gave to them. He only kept for himself and his family a certain amount of money necessary to maintain a dignified lifestyle, and gave away the rest in charity. At his instruction, one of his children donated daily ten pieces of silver to the poor while on Fridays the latter received twenty pieces of silver.

The time one spends with one's children, especially when they are still young, must be punctuated by a maximum of good words, acts and gestures. Imam Abū Ḥanīfah ﵀ encouraged his children to engage in righteous acts hoping it would become a second nature to them. In order to cement in one's children a sense of empathy and understanding towards those who are less fortunate than them, one's children should not be exclusively confined or limited to formal lectures and lessons in sheltered environments. Other environments, such as schools and mosques, should inspire them to engage in voluntary work and charity in the real world.

The other quality that Imam Abū Ḥanīfah ﵀ was also known for is that he never pestered those who owed him money. One man who was struggling to repay Imam Abū Ḥanīfah ﵀ did his best to avoid and hide from him out of shame and shyness. Eventually, when Imam Abū Ḥanīfah ﵀ confronted the man about this peculiar behaviour, he was dumbfounded and asked the man for forgiveness for making him feel the way he did.

Abū Ḥanīfah's ﵀ treatment of those who owed him money shows that one should never treat one's debtor in an obnoxious way or hold a grudge against him, especially if he is earnestly trying his best to pay back his debt. Imam Abū Ḥanīfah ﵀ and all the great servants of this Ummah were known for their strict adherence to the *Dīn*, but at the same time they were very lenient with other people.

Imam Abū ʿAmr al-Shaʿbī, who was known in his community for his affluence and easy-going personality, was naturally inclined to the brilliance of the young businessman, Abū Ḥanīfah. When the Imam asked the latter about his teacher, he said that he had none. Upon which Imam al-Shaʿbī said to him, 'Do not live like a headless man; focus on learning beneficial knowledge, sit [with teachers] within the school. I see within you good qualities.' Imam Abū Ḥanīfah later commented that it was Imam al-Shaʿbī's recognition of his potential that motivated him to seek sacred knowledge.

Oftentimes, one feels that one is not fully appreciated by those who are around him, which inhibits one from exercising one's full potential, and it may also happen that one's surroundings are increasingly dominated by negative criticism and the depreciating of others. Consequently, one forgets how to channel one's talents and skills or even does not bother to try to channel them at all. Imam al-Shaʿbī's encouragement of Abū Ḥanīfah, who was already successful in his business, provides an important lesson. The act of encouraging people to pursue what they are good at is a Prophetic quality, for the Prophet encouraged and nurtured the talents and skills of his Companions as he did, for example, with the writing skills of Zayd ibn Thābit and the beautiful voice of Bilāl ibn Rabāḥ.

KUFA

Located near Najaf in Iraq and established in 15 AH/636 CE, Kufa's history of social and political turbulences enhanced and ripened Imam Abū Ḥanīfah's ﵀ experiences in life. Kufa was at that time one of three major cities in Iraq, the other two being Basra and Baghdad. Saʿd ibn Abī Waqqāṣ ﵁, one of the ten Prophetic Companions promised Paradise (*al-ʿasharah al-mubashsharah bi'l-jannah*), was appointed the governor of Kufa during the Caliphate of ʿUmar ibn al-Khaṭṭāb ﵁ but the Kufans resented this appointment and were unhappy with his governance to the extent that they accused him of governmental abuse. Despite being found innocent, ʿUmar ﵁ recalled Saʿd ﵁ and instead appointed ʿAmmār ibn Yāsir ﵁ as his successor and ʿAbdullāh ibn Masʿūd ﵁ as the chief scholar, which was a difficult sacrifice on the part of ʿUmar ﵁ who loved both of these Companions dearly and wanted to keep them close to him.

Kufa was a garrison city, Muslim soldiers were stationed at the forefront of a growing Islamic empire. Ibn Masʿūd ﵁ was given the responsibility of mentoring the garrison and the city at large, advancing their religious learning and encouraging the community to practise the *Dīn* of the Prophet ﷺ. The people of Kufa took to Ibn Masʿūd ﵁ very well and the city soon began to know a revival in the learning of the Islamic sciences, particularly in the recitation of the Qur'an. Several of the variant recitations of the Qur'an are narrated by the disciples of Ibn Mas'ūd ๛ from Kufa. However, political strife persisted in this city which forced 'Umar to replace his governor there by another Prophetic Companion, al-Mughīrah ibn Sh'ubah ๛.

Kufa was to become a base for rebels who would go on to revolt against 'Uthmān ibn 'Affān ๛ and consequently assassinate him, thus forcing 'Alī ibn Abī Ṭālib ๛ to move the seat of the Islamic Caliphate from Madinah to Kufa. 'Alī ๛ was eventually assassinated by the rebels in the Grand mosque of Kufa. After a brief reign of Ḥasan ibn 'Alī ๛, Mu'āwiyah ibn Abī Sufyān ๛ succeeded him and established the Umayyad dynasty, once again moving the seat of the Caliphate from Kufa to Damascus, Syria. The people of Kufa had always resisted the rule of the Umayyads and contested their legitimacy. Most notably, the people of Kufa offered their city as a refuge for al-Ḥusayn ibn 'Alī ๛ the grandson of the Prophet ﷺ, and his family as a platform to revolt against the rule of Yazīd, the second Umayyad Caliph. Al-Ḥusayn ๛ and his family were ambushed by the army of Yazīd and brutally massacred. From that moment on, the people of Kufa were subjugated to intense scrutiny and control by the Umayyads which bred socio-political frustration in the city.

The Umayyad dynasty ruled from 41 to 130 AH/ 661 to 750 CE and Iraq's frontier proximity exposed it to an influx of political factions, foreign ideas and philosophies that caused division and confusion. In the political realm, prevalent factions included the *Ahl al-Bayt* (the Prophetic Household) and the Abbasids. The *Ahl al-Bayt* were the descendants of ʿAlī ibn Abī Ṭālib while the Abbasids were the descendants of ʿAbdullāh ibn ʿAbbās ﵁, the cousin of the Prophet ﷺ. The Abbasids were involved in several revolts against the Umayyads, eventually overthrowing them in 750 AD during the latter part of Imam Abū Ḥanīfah's ﵀ life. Theological factions and sects included the Khawārij, the Qadariyah, the Muʿtazilah, and remnants of Greco-Roman/Aristotelian philosophical schools all of which deviated in several points of creed from mainstream Sunni beliefs. Discussion of and engagement in politics by the Ulema was forbidden and suppressed by the Umayyads, fearing a popular rebellion due to the injustices and corruption of many of their rulers and kings. Despite all these different theological sects and philosophical schools which were alien to the Islamic ethos, Sunni Islam continued to thrive and be promoted.

Orthodox Sunni beliefs and law continued to be championed by scholars throughout the lands of the Caliphate and especially in Iraq and the Hejaz. Thanks to the descendants of the Prophet ﷺ, and their students who were living in the city, Madinah had preserved the Islamic teachings and Prophetic Practice from the time of the Prophet ﷺ, making it the centre of Hadith studies in the Muslim world. The great scholar and contemporary of Imam Abū Ḥanīfah ﵀, Imam Mālik ibn Anas ﵀, is credited for a compilation of the whole Islamic scholarship of Madinah into what is now called the Mālikī *madhhab*, or school of law. His school is referred to as *ahl al-ḥadīth* (the people of Hadith) or *ahl al-madīnah* (the people of Madinah). The scholars of Iraq were known as *ahl al-ra'y* (the people of opinion). The school of Iraq was known for expanding the use of legal analogy and analysis upon dealing with the sources of Islamic law such as the Qur'an and Hadith in order to refute the dissenters of Kufa. The geographical distance between the two schools gave rise to different legal methodologies. However, the students of both legal schools eventually recognized the advantages of each other's approaches and went on to reach an agreement on many legal points upon which they had differed previously.

SPECIALIZATION IN THEOLOGY

The first focus of Abū Ḥanīfah ☙ upon addressing the theological confusions of the Muslims of Kufa was *'aqīdah* or the tenets of faith. Imam Abū Ḥanīfah ☙ excelled in this discipline and had numerous debates with proponents of unorthodox and aberrant theological views. In this respect, one of the most noteworthy incidents that highlighted Abū Ḥanīfah's ☙ knowledge was his confrontation with a Christian polemicist from Byzantine. In an assembly of Muslim scholars, the man posed three questions: towards where is Allah facing? What was before Allah? And what is Allah doing right now? At a loss on how to respond coherently to this man, Imam Abū Ḥanīfah, ☙ then a young scholar, requested to respond on behalf of the scholars in the audience. On the first question, Imam Abū Ḥanīfah ﷺ lit a candle and asked the man: towards what direction is the light of the candle facing. The man said that the light of the candle was not directed to any particular direction. Abū Ḥanīfah ﷺ pointed out that this was similar to the encompassing reach of Allah. On the second question, Imam Abū Ḥanīfah ﷺ asked the Christian polemicist to count from ten to one. When the man reached number one, Abū Ḥanīfah ﷺ asked him to continue at which the man said he cannot continue. Imam Abū Ḥanīfah ﷺ then said there is no "before" to Allah, for He is the First and the Last, the Outwardly Manifest and the Inwardly Hidden. Before answering the last question, Imam Abū Ḥanīfah ﷺ requested the Christian polemicist to join him on the stage and then had the questioner sit while he spoke. The inquirer obliged and Imam Abū Ḥanīfah ﷺ responded to the last question by saying Allah is currently disgracing the inquirer and giving the upper hand to his opponent who is defending His *Dīn*.

Thus, *ʿaqīdah* was the main interest of Imam Abū Ḥanīfah's ﷺ before he turned his interest to *fiqh*. His book, *al-fiqh al-akbar,* on the tenants of faith is a standard reference on *ʿaqīdah* and is still used to this day as a major source in the study of speculative theology. Imam Abū Ḥanīfah's ﷺ work in the subject of *ʿaqīdah* influenced Imam Abū Jaʿfar al-Ṭaḥāwī, ﷺ the author of the famous Islamic creed, *al-ʿaqīdah hṭaḥāwiyyah*, which is a popular and succinct summation of Sunni tenants of faith.

SPECIALIZATION IN JURISPRUDENCE

During one of his sessions of teaching *ʿaqīdah*, a student approached Imam Abū Ḥanīfah ﷺ and asked him about a point dealing with divorce. Since Imam Abū Ḥanīfah ﷺ had not studied *fiqh* extensively and, therefore, was unqualified to answer that specific question, he referred the student to the great Kufan jurist Ḥammād ibn ʿAlī ibn Abī Sulaymān ﷺ.[42] The question put to Imam Abū Ḥanīfah ﷺ intrigued him and made him long to know the answer and, at the same time, made him realise his shortcomings regarding the vast subject of *fiqh*.

Saying: 'I don't know'as a reposnse to a legitimate question is very honest and absolutely required when one does not know the answer. In fact, it is much better to be truthful about one's ignorance regarding a specific question than feigning a baseless answer. When one does not know the answer to a specific question, it is better to refer the questioner to someone else who knows the answer. Lastly, as the above incident shows, Imam Abū Ḥanīfah wished to learn more when faced with something he did not know. One must make it a point never to stop learning.

Imam Abū Ḥanīfah ﷺ decided there and then to shift his interest and focus to the study of *fiqh*. He studied with his beloved teacher Ḥammād, who was only nine years older than him. Imam Abū Ḥanīfah ﷺ and Ḥammād had great respect and love for each other. When Imam Abū

Ḥanīfah ﷺ first started attending the circle of Ḥammād, he sat at the back of the circle as he was a new student. But after recognizing the genius and commitment of Imam Abū Ḥanīfah ﷺ, Ḥammād made him sit with his senior students in the first row. Imam Abū Ḥanīfah ﷺ advanced quickly in his *fiqh* studies, becoming his teacher's personal assistant, which included accompanying him night and day and carrying his groceries and books. Imam Abū Ḥanīfah ﷺ also did his teacher's housework and tended his garden. He also took questions from the public to his teacher's private quarters. In one instance, Ḥammād had to go to Basra for two months in order to settle a matter of inheritance of a deceased family member. He therefore requested Abū Ḥanīfah ﷺ to temporarily take his place. During these two months, Abū Ḥanīfah ﷺ responded to approximately sixty questions. But upon the return of Hammad, he informed Abū Ḥanīfah ﷺ that he agreed only with forty of his responses. This declaration made Abū Ḥanīfah ﷺ doubt the soundness and solidity of his own knowledge, and he vowed never to leave the tutelage of his teacher.

The believer benefits a great deal, and in countless ways, from serving others and attending to their different needs. Apart from such benefits, attending to the needs and necessities of one's teacher can be a priceless experience that sets one for life and even the afterlife.

ʿAlī ibn Abī Ṭālib ﷺ said, 'I am the slave of whoever teaches me a single word; they can either keep me in bondage or set me free.'

Imam Abū Ḥanīfah's ﷺ personal relationship with his teacher enhanced his mind, body, and soul. His undivided commitment to the service of his teacher was what set him apart from many of his contemporaries. This is the kind of commitment and utter devotion that students of sacred knowledge in the past had for their teachers. They did not merely attend the classes of their teachers and forgot them as soon as they could stand on their own two feet.

Ḥammād passed away at the age of 49 when Abū Ḥanīfah ﷺ was forty years old. Imam Abū Ḥanīfah took his position and met with the community's unanimous acceptance.

HIS QUALITIES

Imam Abū Ḥanīfah ﷺ was renowned for the soundness of his character, piety and righteousness. He was well-known for his humility, intellect and considerable love for his community and students. One of the most distinguished features of Imam Abū Ḥanīfah ﷺ was his devotion to Allah in worship. He was widely known for his long standing in prayer at night (*tahajjud*) and nightly vigils. There are numerous reports about his unwillingness to sleep at night and engagement in forty-day periods of nightly worship. He was widely remembered for being a man of prayer. Indeed, his consistent and humble devotion to Allah at night is what sustained his vigour and strength during the day.

سَمِعْتُ أَبَا نُعَيْمٍ يَقُولُ: «لَقِيتُ الْأَعْمَش ومَسْعَرًا وَحَمْزَةَ الزَّيَّات وَمَالِكَ بن مَغُولٍ وَإِسْرَائِيلَ وَعَمْرو بن ثَابِت وشَرِيكًا وَجَمَاعَة من الْعُلَمَاءِ لَا أُحْصِيهِمْ، فَصَلَّيْتُ مَعَهُمْ فَمَا رَأَيْتُ رَجُلًا أَحْسَنَ صَلَاةٍ مِنْ أَبِي حَنِيفَةَ، وَلَقَد كَانَ قَبْلَ الدُّخُولِ فِي الصَّلَاةِ يَدْعُو وَيسْأَلُ ويَبْكِي، فَيَقُول الْقَائِل هَذَا وَاللهِ يَخْشَى اللهَ».

Abū Nu'aym said: 'I have met countless scholars, including al-A'mash, Mas'ar, Ḥamzah al-Zayyāt, Mālik ibn Maghūl, Isrā'īl, 'Amr ibn Thābit and Sharīk ﵏, yet I have never seen a man with a better and more seemly prayer than that of Abū Ḥanīfah ﵀: before beginning the prayer he would make supplications, ask Allah while crying, in such a way that anyone who saw him would say: "By Allah! This is someone who fears Allah."'

Imam Abū Ḥanīfah ﵀ was very conscious of Allah and his own personal conduct. As a successful businessman, he had the wealth of this *Dunyā* at his fingertips, yet he gave much of it away in charity and chose to pursue a life of service to Allah. A contemporary scholar of Imam Abū Ḥanīfah described the latter as follows:

'He was extremely particular about the unlawful. He avoided many lawful things due to doubt about their lawfulness. I have not encountered a jurist who was more wary about his desires and cautious regarding sacred

> knowledge than him. All of his endeavours were directed for the Hereafter.'

One quality that is exemplified in the life of Imam Abū Ḥanīfah ﵀, and which the students of sacred knowledge nowadays must take to heart, is attachment to Allah Most High and being conscious of even the smallest of things, for what is lawful is clear and what is unlawful is clear, as mentioned in a Prophetic saying.

Imam Abū Ḥanīfah ﵀ had a deep sense of commitment to serving those around him and his community at large. This was very visible in the way he treated his students, perhaps due to his personal relationship with his own teacher, Ḥammād. After accepting any student into his circle, Imam Abū Ḥanīfah ﵀ saw to it that he was properly clothed and given a place to live in. He did the same thing for the student's family. He even communicated marriage proposals on behalf of his students. He also cared for his neighbours and the residents of Kufa. He visited the sick and participated in the funeral prayers over the deceased. One of his senior students, Imam Ẓufar related that Imam Abū Ḥanīfah ﵀ made everyone around him comfortable, regardless of whether the person was rich, poor, ignorant or scholarly. Imam Ẓufar said:

> 'I have never seen anyone who is more willing to listen to people's concerns and then advising them about what to do than Abū Ḥanīfah.'

The great scholars and saints of the past were not hermits. They understood that their service to Islam included scrving their community. They understood that they were the heirs of the Prophet ﷺ and it was their responsibility to be community builders. They enjoyed helping others and kept the company of their peers. Muslims today should emulate their conducts in their communities, such as assisting the needy and visiting the sick, if they want to create a positive image of Islam and bring goodness into society.

Imam Abū Ḥanīfah رحمه الله was the embodiment of several other character traits. He criticised himself first before passing judgement on others. When his gatherings were abruptly interrupted, he did not lash back at whoever did it but patiently waited for them to stop. He listened to his interrupter and saw his interruption as a judgement on himself. Interruptions in his gatherings reminded him not to feel too superior, as there must surely be others who are more knowledgeable than him, and Allah is even more superior in knowledge than all His created beings.

عَنِ ابْنِ الْـمُبَارَكِ قَالَ: «مَا رَأَيْتُ رَجُلًا أَوْقَرَ فِي مَجْلِسِهِ وَلَا أَحْسَنَ سَمْتًا وَحِلْمًا مِنْ أَبِي حنيفَةَ».

'Abdullāh ibn al-Mubārak رحمه الله said: 'I have never seen a man who is more dignified in his gathering nor of better manners and forbearance than Abū Ḥanīfah.'[43]

Thus was Imam Abū Ḥanīfah; he was a man who understood that he was blessed to be a Muslim and did not take this for granted. All his noble character traits were but reflections of his willingness to submit to Allah and the teachings of the Prophet, which enabled him to embody the Prophetic Practice so beautifully and allowed his study of the Islamic sciences to benefit the entire Muslim Ummah to this day.

HIS LEGAL METHODOLOGY AND SCHOOL OF LAW

Imam Abū Ḥanīfah had between thirty-six and forty scholars in his council, each one of them was a master of various Islamic disciplines such as the Arabic language, Hadith, *Tafsīr*, etc. This council discussed legal and theological matters and debated over their respective answers, each scholar giving his perspective based on his expertise while Imam Abū Ḥanīfah presided over these discussions. In fact, many opinions in the Ḥanafī *madhhab* were issued by his students, particularly his two most famous students, *Qāḍī* Abū Yūsuf and Imam Muhammad al-Shaybānī, who went on to develop the Ḥanafī *madhhab* further.

The Imam's personal methodology in answering legal questions was to look first in the Qur'an for answers. If there was no direct answer there, he consulted the *Sunnah* of the Prophet. If he could not find an answer there, he referred to the statements of the Prophetic Companions. If the latter had differed over a question, then Imam Abū Ḥanīfah ﷺ accepted the opinion of the Prophetic Companion that he felt was most in line with his knowledge of the Qur'an and Hadith. However, if he still did not find an answer in the statements of the Prophetic Companions, he issued his own ruling based on his understanding of the religion after consulting the opinions of the students of the Prophetc Companions such as Ibrāhīm al-Nakh'ī and Ḥasan al-Bāṣrī.

LATER LIFE AND POLITICAL TURBULENCE

Like many other scholars, Imam Abū Ḥanīfah was put under tremendous pressure from the governing elite at the height of the conflict between the Umayyads and Abbasids and the latter's overthrow of the former. One of the governors of Kufa attempted to secure Imam Abū Ḥanīfah's loyalty to the Umayyads by appointing him Treasurer or Chief Judge. Imam Abū Ḥanīfah rejected the appointment and was subsequently imprisoned and tortured. He was released with the ultimatum that he would either take the position offered to him or be subjected to more torture. Thereupon, Imam Abū Ḥanīfah fled to Makkah, and it was during his exile in the Hejaz that the two great scholars, Imam Abū Ḥanīfah and Imam Mālik met each other. They engaged in extensive scholarly discussions with one another, which culminated in profound mutual respect for one another. Imam Mālik's students asked whether he had met Imam Abū Ḥanīfah and debated issues with him and his reply was:

'Yes, indeed, I have seen a man who, were he to look at this pillar of stone and state that it was made of gold, he would have been able to argue his case'

سُئِلَ مَالِكُ بْنُ أَنَسٍ: «هَلْ رَأَيْتَ أَبَا حَنِيفَةَ وَنَاظَرْتَهُ؟» فقال: «نَعَمْ!
رَأَيْتُ رَجُلًا لَوْ نَظَرَ إِلَى هَذِهِ السَّارِيَةِ وَهِيَ مِنْ حِجَارَةٍ فَقَالَ إِنَّهَا
مِنْ ذَهَبٍ لَقَامَ بِحُجَّتِهِ».

Imam Abū Ḥanīfah رحمه الله sent his chief student, Imam Abū Yūsuf رحمه الله to study with Imam Mālik رحمه الله. Abū Yūsuf was therefore able to incorporate Imam Mālik's رحمه الله methodology of Hadith in the Ḥanafī *madhhab*. Imam Muhammad al-Shaybānī, رحمه الله another prominent student of Imam Abū Ḥanīfah رحمه الله, also studied with Imam Mālik for three years.

Imam Abū Ḥanīfah رحمه الله remained in the Hejaz for six or seven years. In the year 132 AH/749 CE, when the Abbasids successfully overthrew the Umayyads, he returned to Kufa. The new governor was Abū al-ʿAbbās al-Saffāḥ who was widely known for his hatred of the Umayyads. He gathered the scholars, assured them that the family of the Prophet ﷺ would be taken care of and that freedom of speech is guaranteed for the scholars. Upon which Imam Abū Ḥanīfah responded optimistically by saying:

'All Praise be to Allah who allowed the truth to arise from the family of the Prophet ﷺ and took away the injustice of oppression. We will support you as long as you support the Book of Allah ﷻ and the Sunnah of the Prophet ﷺ.'

The peace did not last, and another governor, Abū Ja'far al-Manṣūr, was named. The latter was a paranoid leader who, upon taking office, offered Imam Abū Ḥanīfah the position of Chief Justice to ensure his loyalty. After declining the offer, Imam Abū Ḥanīfah was thrown in prison once again where he was excessively tortured and left neglected. There is a difference of opinion whether he had succumbed to his wounds in prison, died outside the prison, or whether he was poisoned. What is definitively known is that he passed away at the age of 70 in the year 150 AH/767 CE. In one narration, it was said that Imam Abū Ḥanīfah passed away while in prostration (*sujūd*).

Whether one is a scholar or not, every person is tested at his or her own level and according to his or her ability to withstand the test. Even though he was one of the greatest scholars of his era, Imam Abū Ḥanīfah still suffered incredibly at the hands of his enemies and opponents. However, his ultimate goal was the acceptance of his Lord and Creator, not the acceptance or rejection of other human beings, *Allah charges no soul save to its capacity; standing to its account is what it has earned, and against its account what it has merited.* His life teaches one not to succumb to the temptations of power or politics nor yield to the unreasonable demands of oppressors. The life of Imam Abū Ḥanīfah also shows one how to observe the *Dīn* in all aspects of one's life, even in those aspects that are not seemingly Islamic such as one's career and transactions.

إمام محمد ابن
ادريس الشافعي

Imam Muhammad ibn Idrīs al-Shāfiʿī

The Sea of Knowledge

HIS EARLY LIFE

MUHAMMAD IBN Idrīs al-Shāfiʿī was born in modern day Gaza, Palestine, in 150 AH/767 CE, the same year in which Imam Abū Ḥanīfah passed away. Most historians agree that Imam al-Shāfiʿī was a descendant of ʿAbd al-Manāf through ʿAbd al-Muṭallib, which is the same lineage as that of the Prophet ﷺ. His mother hailed from the Azd clan, although there is a minority opinion which states that she belonged to the Quraysh tribe. Be that as it may, Imam al-Shāfiʿī was known as a Qurashite. At the age of two, al-Shāfiʿī's mother took him to Makkah in an attempt to start his education close to his father's family. Despite his proximity to his relatives in Makkah, al-Shāfiʿī's early years were marked by poverty. This early hardship opened his eyes to the plight of the poor and the downtrodden and his empathy for and identification with these categories of people were vital in his development as a reformer of society. But regardless of poverty, the mother of al-Shāfiʿī ﷬ wanted her son to begin his education by memorizing the Qur'an. Al-Shāfiʿī ﷬ described the sacrifices of his mother as follows:

«كُنْتُ يَتِيمًا فِي حِجْرِ أُمِّي فَدَفَعَتْنِي فِي الكُتَّابِ، وَلَمْ يَكُنْ عِنْدَهَا مَا تعْطِي الـمُعَلِّمَ، فَكَانَ الـمُعَلِّمُ قَدْ رَضِيَ مِنِّي أَنْ أَخْلُفَهُ إِذَا قَامَ، فَلَمَّا خَتَمْتُ القُرْآنَ دَخَلْتُ الـمَسْجِدَ، فَكُنْتُ أُجَالِسُ العُلَمَاءَ، وَكُنْتُ أَسْمَعُ الحَدِيثَ أَوْ الـمَسْأَلَةَ فَأَحْفَظُهَا، وَلَمْ يَكُنْ عِنْدَ أُمِّي مَا تُعْطِينِي أَنْ أَشْتَرِيَ بِهِ قَرَاطِيسَ قَطُّ، فَكُنْتُ إِذَا رَأَيْتُ عَظْمًا يَلُوحُ آخُذُهُ فَأَكْتُبُ فِيهِ، فَإِذَا امْتَلَأَ طَرَحْتُهُ فِي جَرَّةٍ كَانَتْ لَنَا قَدِيمَةٍ».

'I was an orphan living with my mother when she sent me to the Qur'anic school. However, she did not have anything with which she could pay the teacher, and so the teacher accepted to teach me provided that I stand for him when he had to attend to some of his business. When I finished the memorisation of the Quran, I went to the mosque and started attending the sessions of different scholars. I used to hear a Prophetic narration or a question of knowledge and straightaway memorized it. At that time my mother did not have any money to give me to buy parchments, so whenever I found any

animal bones I took them to write on, and
when there was no more space in them to write
on, I placed them in an old jar of ours.'[44]

Imam al-Shāfiʿī's ❦ experience of living in poverty
shows that material poverty is not a disgrace and, in fact,
the Prophet, peace and blessings be upon him, did not
have any material wealth. It also teaches that one should
not look down on people just because they are poor or
destitute, as they might be of great consequence in the
eyes of Allah. How many a poor person went on to change
his society and even the world. The perseverance and
determination of al-Shāfiʿī's mother ❦ is also admirable,
for it was her sacricife and selfless struggle that, in the
final account, determined the career of Imam al-Shāfiʿī.
She could have directed her child to any other field,
especially since they were very poor, but she chose for him
learning the *Dīn*. No one should look down on those who
give their religion a higher priority over what society may
deem to be the natural course to follow by everyone if they
wish to be accepted as normal or not be labelled as weird.
When parents give priority to the *Dīn* in the upbringing
of their children, Allah takes care of their children in
unpredictable and unexpected ways.

Although al-Shāfiʿī's mother ❦ did not have any
money to pay for his lessons and despite her strained
financial circumstances, Allah made it easy for the young
al-Shāfiʿī to pursue his studies unhindered.

قَالَ الشَّافِعِيّ: «كُنْتُ وَأَنَا فِي الكُتَّابِ أَسْمَعُ المُعَلِّمَ يُلَقِّنُ الصَّبِيَّ الآيَةَ فَأَحْفَظُهَا أَنَا، وَلَقَدْ كَانَ الصِّبْيَانُ يَكْتُبُونَ أَمْلِيَتَهُمْ فَإِلَى أَنْ يَفْرَغَ المُعَلِّمُ مِنَ الإِمْلاءِ عَلَيْهِمْ قَدْ حَفِظْتُ جَمِيعَ مَا أَمْلَى. فَقَالَ لِي ذَاتَ يَوْمٍ: مَا يَحِلُّ لِي أَنْ آخُذَ مِنْكَ شَيْئًا».

Imam al-Shāfiʿī said: 'When I was learning in the Qur'anic school, I memorised whatever the teacher was repeating to any child there to memorise. By the time the other children finished writing their dictations, I had all their dictations memorised. Seeing this, my teacher said to me one day: 'It is not illicit for me to take any payment from you.'[45]

In Makkah, the young al-Shāfiʿī stood out from amongst his peers for his intelligence, memory and sharpness. He quickly memorized the Holy Qur'an by the age of seven. After that, he proceeded to memorize the traditions of the Prophet. Due to his mother's prompting, he sought the most authoritative scholars of *fiqh* and Hadith in Makkah such as Sufyān ibn ʿUyaynah and Isḥāq ibn Rahwayh. Imam al-Shāfiʿī was granted the authorisation to respond to legal questions in his early to mid-teens.

FURTHER STUDIES

In Makkah, Imam al-Shāfiʿī was able to gain mastery in all the Islamic sciences by the time he reached his twentieth year. He spent time living among the Bedouin tribes and learnt their different dialects, thus becoming an authority in the Arabic language in all its different disciplines, such as grammar, syntax, rhetoric, etc. He also became a prolific poet as well as an expert in the pre-Islamic pagan poetry. While living with the Bedouins, he also learnt horse riding and archery. When he returned to Makkah from his time with the Bedouins, he often recited poetry. One day, after hearing him recite poems, a relative of his said to him:

«يَا أَبَا عَبْدَ الله، عَزَّ عَلَيَّ أَنْ لَا يَكُونَ مَعَ هَذِهِ الفَصَاحَةِ وَالذَّكَاءِ فِقْهٌ، فَتَكُونَ قَدْ سُدْتَ أَهْلَ زَمَانِكَ. فَقُلْتُ: فَمَنْ بَقِيَ مِمَّا يَقْصُدُ؟ فَقَالَ لِي: هَذَا مَالِكٌ سَيِّدُ الـمُسْلِمِينَ يَوْمَئِذٍ. فَوَقَعَ فِي قَلْبِي، وَعَمِدْتُ إِلَى الـمَوَطَّأ فَاسْتَعْرَضْتُهُ وَحَفِظْتُهُ فِي تِسْعِ لَيَالٍ».

"O Abū ʿAbdullāh! It pains me that such eloquence and intelligence is without *fiqh*, for if you had it you would become the master of your contemporaries.' Al-Shāfiʿī ﷺ responded: 'Who is still alive from among the scholars who deserve to be sought?' He said: 'There is Mālik ibn Anas, the master of the Muslims nowadays'. Al-Shāfiʿī ﷺ said: 'I took his words to heart, I got a copy of the *Muwaṭṭa'* and memorized it in nine days.'[46]

After getting all the knowledge he could get in Makkah in his early twenties, he travelled to Madinah to study under the esteemed Imam Mālik ﷺ. Imam Mālik ﷺ was widely regarded as the foremost expert on Hadith, Islamic jurisprudence and Islamic knowledge in general.

This great scholar was known for his striking demeanour and stern personality and this made even government officials avoid asking him for anything out of awe. However, in order to help al-Shāfiʿī ﷺ in his journey, the governor of Madinah sent with him a letter to Imam Mālik ﷺ, hoping that Imam Malik ﷺ would take special care of this precocious student. Feeling insulted by this attempt, Imam Mālik ﷺ threw the letter and said:

«سُبْحَانَ اللهِ! وَصَارَ عِلْمُ رَسُولِ اللهِ ﷺ يُؤْخَذُ بِالوَسَائِلِ».

'Glory be to Allah! The knowledge of the Prophet, peace and blessings be upon him, is now obtained through connections!'[47]

However, Imam Mālik ﷺ became quickly aware of al-Shāfiʿī's ﷺ remarkable intelligence and memory. He asked al-Shāfiʿī to read the *Muwaṭṭa'* to him from memory and was pleasantly surprised at his beautiful and accurate reading of the Prophetic traditions narrated by Imam Mālik ﷺ . In only a few days, they completed the reading of the entire *Muwaṭṭa'*.

During the time he spent as a student of Imam Mālik ﷺ, Imam al-Shāfiʿī ﷺ turned his attention to the study of *fiqh*. He remained in Madinah with Imam Mālik ﷺ for nearly nine years until Imam Mālik's ﷺ death in 179 AH/795 CE. While studying in Madinah, al-Shāfiʿī ﷺ visited Makkah to see his mother and his old teachers towards whom he showed great love and respect. After the death of Imam Mālik ﷺ, he continued his studies across the Muslim world, and his frequent travels allowed him to observe the situation of the Muslim Ummah. Among his most notable travels were his journeys to Yemen and Iraq. While in Yemen, Imam al-Shāfiʿī's ﷺ teaching career took off and he quickly gained a very large following due to his mastery of jurisprudence based on the Qur'an and Hadith. In Yemen, Imam al-Shāfiʿī ﷺ became embroiled in legal issues while serving as a government official. He was also accused by some sectarian factions of being a deviant person and conspirator against the state. Thus, at the age of thirty-four, he was wrongfully accused of attempting to overthrow the government of the day and was dispatched to Baghdad, the Caliphate's capital, to face trial.

IRAQ AND IMAM MUHAMMAD

In the court of Caliph Hārūn al-Rashīd ﷺ, Imam al-Shāfiʿī ﷺ vehemently defended his innocence. Undecided about al-Shāfiʿī's innocence, Hārūn al-Rashīd ﷺ turned to his adviser, Imam Muhammad ibn al-Ḥasan al-Shaybānī, ﷺ to seek his opinion about the matter. Imam Muhammad testified that al-Shāfiʿī was a a man of truth, piety and honour and he must have been wrongfully accused. This was enough to secure his release. Imam Muhammad al-Shaybā nī ﷺ was one of Imam Abū Ḥanīfah's ﷺ foremost students and many of his writings and legal opinions contributed to codifying the principles and method of the Ḥanafī school of law. Following his acquittal, a natural bond of love and respect developed between Imam al-Shāfiʿī ﷺ and Imam Muhammad ﷺ and the latter welcomed the former at his home. Imam al-Shāfiʿī ﷺ went on to study under Imam

Muhammad ﷺ for five years, during which he transcribed and studied his books in depth all while holding debates with him and with his foremost students. The time he spent in Baghdad allowed him to gain a deeper understanding of the method of the school of *Ahl-al-Ra'y*, a method which relies on the use of opinion, legal analogy and analysis more than it does on the transmission of narrations. After the death of Imam Muhammad ﷺ in 189 AH/805 CE, Imam al-Shāfiʿī ﷺ returned to Makkah and taught in *al-Masjid al-Ḥarām* for nine years. During this time, he developed his own methodology for interpreting the texts of the Sacred Law. His relocation to Makkah from Iraq freed him from the need to respond to and refute heterodox tenants of faith, which were then rife there, especially in Kufa.

It was in Makkah that Imam al-Shāfiʿī ﷺ met the great scholar Imam Aḥmad ibn Ḥanbal ﷺ during the latter's trip to perform the *Ḥajj*. Imam Aḥmad ﷺ remarked later that Imam al-Shāfiʿī ﷺ had the expertise to understand the Holy Qur'an and Hadith and then extrapolate rulings when there were no unified or codified principles and guidelines on how to do so. Therefore, in order to clarify the processes followed in answering legal questions, he developed universal principles that constitute a general framework for the deduction of legal rulings. He laid out this legal framework in his major work, *Kitāb al-Risālah*, which he made public during his second visit to Iraq in 195 AH/810 CE. In Iraq, Imam al-Shāfiʿī ﷺ disseminated his legal theory which marked a significant advance in the study and teaching of *fiqh*. His legal method also helped to bridge the gap between the *fiqh* of the Hejaz and that of Iraq. As Imam Ahmad ﷺ himself stated:

قَالَ أَحْمَدُ : «وَكُنَّا نَلْعَنُ أَصْحَابَ الرَّأْيِ وَيَلْعُونَنَا حَتَّى جَاءَ الشَّافِعِيُّ فَمَزَجَ بَيْنَنَا».

Imam Aḥmad said: 'We used to curse the *Ahl al-Ra'y* (Iraq) and they us until al-Shāfiʿī came along and combined the legal methods of both schools.'[48]

HIS QUALITIES

Along with being a steadfast lover of Allah and His Messenger ﷺ, Imam al-Shāfiʿī ﷺ stood out in the annals of Islamic scholarship as someone who bridged different scholarly methodologies.[49] His impoverishment in early life and travels across the Muslim world marked his incredible personality. He was full of empathy and tolerance which he used to build bridges between the different juristic schools. The Imam studied under different teachers who had different methodologies and in diverse locations but he had a high capacity for independent thought. The respect and high esteem he had for his teachers, however, did not prevent him from respectfully refuting some of their positions, as he did with Imam Mālik ﷺ and Imam Muhammad ﷺ.

قَالَ يُونُسُ الصَّدَفِيُّ: «مَا رَأَيْتُ أَعْقَلَ مِنَ الشَّافِعِيِّ: نَاظَرْتُهُ يَوْماً فِي مَسْأَلَةٍ ثُمَّ افْتَرَقْنَا وَلَقِيَنِي، فَأَخَذَ بِيَدِي ثُمَّ قَالَ: يَا أَبَا مُوسَى أَلَا يَسْتَقِيمُ أَنْ نَكُونَ إِخْوَاناً وَإِنْ لَمْ نَتَّفِقْ فِي مَسْأَلَةٍ».

> Yūnus al-Ṣadafī said: 'I have not seen anyone more reasonable than al-Shāfiʿī: we had a debate one day about a certain issue and then we left. When we met again, he took me by the hand and said: 'O Abū Mūsā (his agnomen), is it not right that we should be brothers even if we differ about a certain issue?'[50]

Communities do not break up over the disagreements that happen in their midst but they may do due to the ways they choose to conduct these disagreements. Imam al-Shāfiʿī ﵀ is held in high regards and esteem because of the way he differed with his opponents. One has to be emotionally and psychologically mature such that one can disagree with another person without being angry or keeping a grudge against him or her. Falling out with others is often less to do with the arguments that people have and more with their egos. Al-Shāfiʿī's ﵀ disagreements with other scholars were not personal but rather a genuine attempt to interprept the Sacred Law which happened to differ from the genuine attempts of other great scholars.

The Imam's keenness on giving to charity is another one of his famous character traits, most likely due to his own financial hardship not just in childhood but even during his travels. Imam al-Shāfiʿī ﵀ embodied a balanced approach between giving to charity and disseminating knowledge as an essential part of his personality and approach. His relationships were not built or broken on any foundation other than the love of Allah Most High and His beloved Messenger, peace and blessings be upon him. The Prophet, peace and blessings be upon him, said:

مَنْ أَحَبَّ للهِ وَأَبْغَضَ للهِ وَأَعْطَى للهِ وَمَنَعَ للهِ فَقَدِ اسْتَكْمَلَ الإِيمَانَ

'Whosover loves for Allah's sake, loathes for Allah's sake, gives for Allah's sake and withholds for Allah's sake has perfected [his] faith.

Imam al-Shāfiʿī practised this Prophetic teaching all his life. Generosity is not confined to giving from one's wealth, it is rather giving to others whatever one possesses, whether it is material possession or something else. Imam al-Shāfiʿī ﷺ was known for his altruism despite having little money. Indeed, providing wisdom, good company and a cheerful mien to others is the ultimate charity. Giving to others what one cherishes most is a sign of true piety.

لَنْ تَنَالُوا الْبِرَّ حَتَّى تُنْفِقُوا مِمَّا تُحِبُّونَ وَمَا تُنْفِقُوا مِنْ شَيْءٍ
فَإِنَّ اللهَ بِهِ عَلِيمٌ

You will not attain piety until you expend of what you love; and whatever thing you expend, Allah knows of it.[51]

قَالَ ابْنُ عَبْدِ الحَكَمِ: «كَانَ الشَّافِعِيُّ أَسْخَى النَّاسِ بِمَا يَجِدُ وَكَانَ يَمُرُّ بِنَا فَإِنْ وَجَدَنِي وَإِلاَّ قَالَ: قُولُوا لِمُحَمَّدٍ إِذَا جَاءَ يَأْتِي المَنْزِلَ فَإِنِّي لاَ أَتَغَدَّى حَتَّى يَجِيءَ».

Ibn ʿAbd al-Ḥakam said: ʿAl-Shāfiʿī ﵀ was the most generous of people regarding what he possessed. He would pass by us and invite me to eat with him, and when he didn't find me at home, he would say to those present: ʿWhen Muhammad comes back, tell him to come to my house, for I will not have lunch until he comes.'[52]

قَالَ الشَّافِعِيُّ: «... فَقَبَضْتُ الأَرْبَعِينَ أَلْفٍ وَخَرَجْتُ مِنْ مَدِينَةِ حَرَّانَ وَبَيْنَ يَدَيَّ أَحْمَالُ الدَّنَانِيرِ والدَّرَاهِمِ يَلْقَانِي الرِّجَالُ وَأَصَحَابُ الحَدِّيثِ مِنْهُمْ أَحْمَدُ بْن حَنْبَل وَسُفْيَان بْن عُيَيْنَة وَالأَوْزَاعِيّ. فَمَا زِلْتُ أُجِيزُ كُلَّ إِنْسَانٍ مِنْهُم عَلَى قَدْرِ مَا قُسِمَ لَهُ وَمَعْرِفَتِهِ حَتَّى دَخَلْتُ مَدِينَةَ الرَّمْلَةِ وَلَيْسَ مَعِي إِلَّا عَشْرَةَ دَنَانِيرَ فَاشْتَرَيْتُ بِهَا رَاحِلَةً وَاسْتَوَيْتُ عَلَى كُورِهَا وَقَصَدْتُ الحِجَازَ».

Imam al-Shāfiʿī ﵀ said: ʿ... and so I received forty thousands and left the city of Ḥarrān: with loads of gold and silver pieces ahead of me. Whenever I met men and scholars of Hadith, such as Aḥmad ibn Ḥanbal, ﵀ Sufyān ibn ʿUyaynah ﵀, and al-Awzaʿī, ﵀ I gave each one of them according to what was apportioned for him and in commensuration with his knowledge until I entered the city of Ramlah with only ten gold pieces in my possession. I therefore used it to buy a mount, mounted it and set out for the Hejaz.'[53]

Imam al-Shāfiʿī's ﷺ embodiment of these qualities teaches one how one's relationship with Allah cannot be correct and thriving unless one deals with people in the most gracious and kind manner.

LATER LIFE IN EGYPT

In 199 AH/814 CE, Imam al-Shāfiʿī ﷺ had to flee from Egypt when the Caliph al-Ma'mūn coerced all scholars to sanction and promote the Mu'tazilite beliefs.[54] Egypt, for Imam al-Shāfiʿī, ﷺ was a completely different experience as he encountered a new culture that was different from Muslim culture in the Hejaz and Iraq. This fact made him revise some of his legal opinions to better reflect the conditions and circumstances of the Egyptian people. Despite some resistance, he dramatically gained the affection and trust of the Egyptian masses and his students were mesmerized with his eclectic and diverse background in Islamic scholarship. As is described by one of his students, al-Rabīʿ ibn Sulaymān:

قَالَ الرَّبِيعُ بْن سُلَيْمَان: «كَانَ الشَّافِعِيُّ رَحِمَهُ اللهُ يَجْلِسُ فِي حَلَقَتِهِ إِذَا صَلَّى الصُّبْحَ فَيَجِيئُهُ أَهْلُ القُرْآنِ، فَإِذَا طَلَعَتِ الشَّمْسُ قَامُوا وَجَاءَ أَهْلُ الحَدِيثِ فَيَسْأَلُونَهُ تَفْسِيرَهُ وَمَعَانِيه، فَإِذَا إِرْتَفَعَتِ الشَّمْسُ قَامُوا فَاسْتَوَتْ الحَلَقَةُ لِلْمُذَاكَرَةِ وَالنَّظَرِ، فَإِذَا إِرْتَفَعَ الضُّحَى تَفَرَّقُوا وَجَاءَ أَهْلُ العَرَبِيَّةِ وَالعَرُوضِ وَالنَّحْوِ وَالشِّعْرِ فَلَا يَزَالُونَ إِلَى قُرْبِ إِنْتِصَافِ النَّهَارِ ثُمَّ يَنْصَرِفُ رَضِيَ اللهُ عَنْهُ».

> Al-Rabīʿ ibn Sulaymān said: ʻal-Shāfiʿī ﷺ used to sit for his study circle after performing the *Ṣubḥ* prayer. The folk of the Qur'an came first to study with him until sunrise. At sunrise they left and the students of Hadith came after them to ask him about its interpretation and meanings until the sun rose high in the horizon. After they had left, the study circle would turn to discussing different questions and issues until midmorning when they would disperse. Then the people of the Arabic language, prosody, grammar and poetry came to study with him. They studied with him until around midday, upon which he would get up and leave.'[55]

His life's work evolved into one of the four schools of Islamic jurisprudence. The *Shāfiʿī madhhab* is mainly observed in Egypt, Yemen, the Levant, the Middle East, and Maritime Southeast Asia. The final years of Imam al-Shāfiʿī' ﷺ were stressful. He dealt with physically-taxing illnesses that led to his death. He passed away on the last day of Rajab at the age of 54 in 204 AH/819 CE.

إمام احمد
ابن حنبل

Imam Aḥmad ibn Ḥanbal

The Reviver of the Sunnah

EARLY LIFE

HIS FULL name is Aḥmad ibn Muhammad ibn Ḥanbal Abū ʿAbdullāh al-Shaybānī al-Marwazī. ﵀ He was born in 164 AH/780 CE in the city of Baghdad, Iraq. His family hailed from the Arab tribe of Shaybān, which according to Shaykh Abū Ḥasan Alī Nadwī ﵀, 'was renowned for its courage, endurance, grit, and vigour.'[56] His grandfather was an Umayyad governor sympathetic to the Abbasid movement. After the death of Imam Aḥmad's father, ﵀ his mother moved to Basra where Aḥmad was born.

His pious mother placed the young child in the company of the ulema of Baghdad during the day while she attended to her own activities in the women's area of the mosque. From an early age, Imam Aḥmad ﵀ surpassed his peers in academic achievement. During his time in Baghdad, he memorised the Qur'an, attended classes of fiqh and Hadith, studied literature and worked in the postal office. His self-imposed discipline and adherence to the prescriptions of the *Sharīʿah* were meticulous. The young Aḥmad discarded letters he was obliged to deliver because he believed they contained secret reports on certain people.

His family lived a simple life, having only inherited a small property from his extended family. Despite their straitened financial situation, Imam Aḥmad ﵀ was very close to his mother. He never travelled by sea while his mother was still alive because she worried too much about him travelling by sea. His devotion to his mother was such that he abstained from marriage in order to be completely devoted to the service of his mother. These noble qualities of respect, honour and intense love for one's mother are always present among the great men of Islamic history. But this should not be a surprise to anyone as these qualities are inherited from the Prophet Muhammad ﷺ and his devotion to the memory of his mother Āminah ﵂ and his foster mother Ḥalīmah ﵂. From the age of fifteen, Imam Aḥmad ﵀ spent approximately twenty years in Baghdad learning the Islamic sciences, with a special focus on Hadith. He could not wait to leave his home before the break of dawn to begin his study. His mother used to beg him to wait at least until the *adhān* before leaving. Some of his teachers in Baghdad included Abū Bakr ibn ʿAyyāsh, Haytham ibn Bashīr, *Qāḍī* Abū Yūsuf as well as other scholars of Hadith. This helped him later to lay down the outlines of his *fiqh* methodology which was versatile but avoided the use of legal analogy of (*qiyās*). Indeed,

Imam Aḥmad ﷺ was exposed to different perspectives on Islamic law and theology. These perspectives included those of *Ahl al-Ra'y* (the people of opinion) whose *fiqh* was codified by Imam Abū Ḥanīfah ﷺ and *Ahl al-Ḥadīth* (the people of Hadith) whose *fiqh* was codified by Imam Mālik ibn Anas ﷺ. After compeleting his studies in Baghdad, he travelled across the Muslim world to acquire further knowledge and collect Hadith. He first travelled to Kufa and Basra in Iraq, then to the Hejaz, Yemen and Syria, learning in the process from the likes of Waqīʿ ibn al-Jarrāḥ and ʿAbd al-Raḥmān ibn Mahdī.

When nearing his mid-twenties, Imam Ahmad ﷺ came into contact with the great jurist Muhammad ibn Idrīs-al-Shāfiʿī ﷺ the founder of the Shāfiʿī *Madhhab*. The two became fond of each other and had mutual admiration for one another, with Imam al-Shāfiʿī ﷺ attesting to Imam Ahmad's ﷺ mastery in the discipline of Hadith and Imam Aḥmad ﷺ attesting to Imam al-Shāfiʿī's ﷺ mastery of Islamic law. Imam al-Shāfiʿī said,

قَـــالَ الشَّـــافِعِيّ: «خَرَجْتُ مِنَ العِرَاقِ فَمَا تَرَكْتُ رَجُلًا أَفْضَلَ وَلَا أَعْلَمَ وَلَا أَوْرَعَ وَلَا أَتْقَى مِنْ أَحْمَد بْن حَنْبَل».

Imam al-Shāfiʿī said: 'I departed from Iraq and I have not left there a man who is better, more knowledgeable, more godfearing or more pious than Aḥmad Ibn Ḥanbal.'[57]

MU'TAZILISM AND THE MIḤNAH

From approximately 195 to 232 AH/810 to 847 CE, during the Abbasid Caliphate, a school of Islamic thought called Mu'tazilism emerged in Baghdad. Mu'tazilism adopted the rational and philosophical thought of the Greeks and applied it on Islamic theology and law. Essentially, the school gave precedence to reason over scriptural texts in questions relating to tenets of faith. Obviously, such an approach contradicted the Sunni Orthodox stance which gives precedence to scriptural proofs over reason.

The believers may not be capable of understanding everything that Allah Most High has revealed. They are, however, required to reflect with open minds on the Divine commandments, injunction and teachings and hear and obey. The major flaw of Mu'tazilism was its attempt to limit the attributes of Allah within the confines of human reason.

One of the main positions of the Mu'tazilites was that the Qur'an is created rather than being Allah's eternal Word. Sunni orthodoxy maintains that the Qur'an is the eternal and uncreated Speech of Allah. Imam Ahmad ﵀ and many of his contemporary Sunni scholars rejected this Mu'tazilite heresy and argued against it.

The Abbasid caliph al-Ma'mūn, who was a staunch supporter of Mu'tazilite doctrines wanted these doctrines to be the new official creed of the Muslim Ummah. In order to achieve this, he decreed that all scholars had to announce their belief in them and renounce the belief in the uncretedness of the Qur'an. This episode in Islamic history is known as the *miḥnah* or "The Great Trial". Many of the scholars yielded to the caliph's pressure, either out of conviction or expediency.

However, when the governor of Baghdad gathered the ulema and questioned them about their stance regarding the Mu'tazilite doctrines, they rejected them. Al-Ma'mūn angrily ordered two of these scholars to be executed and the seven others to be sent to him so that he questions them personally. Three days later, two of these scholars were coerced into changing their stance, only Imam Aḥmad ⚜ and four others from Baghdad championed the traditionalist orthodox belief in the uncreatedness of the Qur'an. Imam Aḥmad ⚜ and Muhammad ibn Nūḥ as well as nineteen other ulema from across the Muslim caliphate were sent to al-Ma'mūn for questioning. While on their way to his court, al-Ma'mūn passed away and both Imam Ahmad ⚜ and Ibn Nuḥ were redirected to Baghdad, and Ibn Nūḥ passed away during this journey back to Baghdad.

However, the death of al-Ma'mūn did not put an end to the *miḥnah*, as his successor, al-Mu'taṣim kept the *miḥnah* going for he, too, believed in the Mu'tazilite doctrines. Imam Aḥmad was brought before the governor of Baghdad and ordered to accept and sanction the doctrine of the createdness of the Qur'an which was championed by the Caliph. He refused and was therefore sent to al-Mu'taṣim. He was then severely tortured and whipped but he refused to accept the Mu'tazilite heresy which was contrary to the teachings brought by the Prophet ﷺ.

After spending over two years in prison, Imam Ahmad was released which allowed him to return home. His steadfastness and defiance of the regime and its new deviant beliefs dealt a crippling blow to the advocates of Mu'tazilism and their heretical beliefs and Sunni orthodoxy emerged triumphant. Al-Mutawakkil, the next major caliph, restored Sunni orthodox beliefs about the Qur'an as a state policy and Imam Aḥmad emerged as a defender and champion of Islam and Islamic orthodoxy.

HIS QUALITIES

Apart from the major and leading role he played during this unpleasant episode in Islamic history, Imam Aḥmad ibn Ḥanbal's ﵀ contribution to Islamic knowledge and scholarship is immense. As a reaction against the widespread of Mu'tazilism, he directed scholarly attention to the absolute importance of the primary sources of Islamic thought: the Quran and Hadith. Imam Aḥmad ibn Ḥanbal's ﵀ approach focused more on the literal purports of the Qur'an and Hadith in seeking legal rulings for any questions, whereby the use of reason was limited. His approach highlighted that the Qur'an and Hadith were broad enough to address any questions or issues, without the need for the Mu'tazilite's excessive use of reason.

قال عبدُ الـمَلِك الـمَيمُونِيّ: «ما رَأَتْ عَيْنِي أَفْضَلَ مِنْ أَحْمَدَ بْن حَنْبَلَ، وَمَا رَأَيْتُ أَحَدًا مِنَ الـمُحَدِّثِينَ أَشَدَ تَعْظِيماً لِحُرُمَاتِ اللهِ عَزَّ وَجَلَّ وَسُنَةِ نَبِيِّهِ ﷺ إِذَا صَحَّتْ عِنْدَهُ وَلَا أَشَدَّ اتِّبَاعاً مِنْهُ».

'Abd al-Malik al-Maymūnī said: 'My eyes have not seen anyone better than Aḥmad ibn Ḥanbal, ﵀ nor have I seen any scholar of Hadith who had more exaltation for what Allah has made inviolable and for the Sunnah of His Prophet ﷺ , if he found it to be authentic, nor yet anyone who followed the sunnah more than him'.[58]

وقَالَ عَبْدُ الوَهَّابِ الوَرَّاق: «مَا رَأَيْتُ مِثْلَ أَحْمَد بْن حَنْبَل - رَحْمَةُ اللهِ عَلَيْهِ». قالُوا لَهُ: «وَأَيْش الَّذِي كانَ مِن فَضْلِهِ وعِلْمِهِ عَلى سَائِرِ مَنْ رَأَيْتَ؟» قَالَ: «رَجُلٌ سُئِلَ عَنْ سِتِّينَ أَلْفَ مَسْأَلَةٍ فَأَجابَ عَنْها بِأَنْ قَالَ: حَدَّثَنا وَأَخبَرَنا».

'Abd al-Wahhāb al-Warrāq said: 'I have not seen anyone like Aḥmad Ibn Ḥanbal ﵀ .' He was asked: "What is it about his knowledge and virtue that have made him stand above all those you have seen?' He said: 'He was a man who was asked about sixty thousand questions and only answered by saying: "So and so narrated to us, and so and so related to us [ie. only through the mention of Prophetic reports)."'[59]

Qāḍī Abū Yūsuf, one of the foremost students of Imam Abū Ḥanīfah ﷺ, was the first teacher of Imam Aḥmad ibn Ḥanbal ﷺ in Baghdad while his other great teacher was Imam al-Shāfiʿī. ﷺ It was during this time that Imam Aḥmad ﷺ began compiling one of the most famous and widely-used collections of Hadith, which he titled *al-Musnad.* This collection of Hadith is one of the most important collections of Hadith which is commonly studied along with the other five Hadith collections, *al-Ṣiḥāḥ al-Sittah*. Starting with Abū Bakr ﷺ, he listed all the narrations related by the Prophetic Companions in order of their seniority. The *Musnad* lists a total of thirty thousand traditions. Eventually, Imam Aḥmad's great wisdom and his fusion of Hadith with his own study of the Ḥanafī and Shāfiʿī schools of law enabled him to found the fourth school of Islamic jurisprudence, the Ḥanbalī *madhhab*.

قَالَ أَبُو القَاسِمِ بْن الجُبُّلِي: «كَانَ أَحْمَدُ بْن حَنْبَل إِذَا سُئِلَ عَنِ المَسْأَلَةِ كَأَنَّ عِلْمَ الدُّنْيَا بَيْنَ عَيْنَيْهِ».

Abū al-Qāsim al-Jubbulī said: 'When Imam Aḥmad ibn Ḥanbal was asked about a question, it was as if the knowledge of the whole world was in front of his eyes.'[60]

However, despite Imam Aḥmad's stoic personality, he epitomized the trait of forgiveness. Following his imprisonment and torture by the Caliph al-Muʿtaṣim, he had to undergo some medical treatment to help him recover from the ordeal he went through but he refused any sort of anesthetic, opting instead to pull a pillow to his chest. His son, Ṣāliḥ, observed that his lips were constantly moving during the treatment. When he later asked his father what he was reciting. Surprisingly, Imam Aḥmad ﷺ replied that he was fearful of passing away during the treatment and therefore he was praying for the forgiveness of Caliph al-Muʿtaṣim. He then narrated the following hadith:

رَوَى ابْنُ الْمُبَارَكِ قالَ: حَدَّثَنِي مَن سَمِعَ الحَسَنَ يَقُولُ: «إِذَا جَاءَتْ الأُمَمُ بَيْنَ يَدَيْ رَبِّ العالَمِينَ يَوْمَ القِيامَةِ نُودِيَ لِيَقُمْ مَن أَجْرُهُ عَلى اللهِ فَلا يَقُومُ إِلَّا مَن عَفَا فِي الدُّنْيا»، يُصَدِّقُ هَذا الحَدِيثَ قَوْلُهُ تَعالَى: «فَمَن عَفَا وأَصْلَحَ فَأَجْرُهُ عَلى اللهِ (الشورى ٤٠)».

Ibn al-Mubārak related that he heard someone who heard al-Ḥasan al-Baṣrī ﷺ say: 'When the nations are gathered before the Lord of the worlds on the Day of Judgment, it will be called out: "Let him who has consigned his reward to Allah stand up!". And none shall stand up except the one who has forgiven others in the worldly life.' This report is confirmed by the Qur'anic verse: (Whoever forgives and pardons for their reward is upon Allah).'[61]

What can possibly motivate a person to seek forgiveness for someone who has pushed him to near death? A person who has imprisoned, flogged and tortured him? People often think that forgiveness is for the one who has asked for it, perhaps as a means of finding peace and closure. However, this does not need to be always the case as Islam permeates all aspects life, and the quality of forgiveness is part of it. Forgiveness is pleasing to Allah Most High and His Messenger ﷺ. In the case of al-Muʿtaṣim, asking forgiveness for him was not a favour to the Caliph but rather a means of pleasing Allah.

عَنْ عَبْدِ اللهِ بْنِ عَمْرٍو يَبْلُغُ بِهِ النَّبِيَّ ﷺ: «الرَّاحِمُونَ يَرْحَمُهُمُ الرَّحْمَنُ: اِرْحَمُوا أَهْلَ الأَرْضِ يَرْحَمْكُمْ مَنْ فِي السَّماءِ».

ʿAbdullāh ibn ʿAmr ibn Al-ʿĀṣ ‎رضي الله عنه‎ narrated that the Prophet ﷺ said: 'The merciful amongst people are shown mercy by the All-Merciful. Show mercy to the inhabitants of the earth and the One in heaven will show mercy to you.'[62]

Apart from his keenness to please Allah Most High and His Messenger ﷺ, Imam Aḥmad ibn Ḥanbal ‎رحمه الله‎ was unattached to the material possession of this world. He maintained that attachment to material things weakened one's connection with Allah and argued that the slightest inclination to unnecessary commodities was detrimental to one's spiritual state. After the *Miḥnah* was over, his son related that the office of the Caliph sent money as an amend for what had happened to him but the Imam refused to accept it. It is also noteworthy that he also refused the gifts presented to him by his students.

قَالَ صَالِحٌ: قُلْتُ لِأَبِي: إِنَّ أَحْمَدَ الدَّوْرَقِيَّ أُعْطِيَ أَلْفَ دِينَارٍ فَقَالَ: يا بُنَيَّ: «وَرِزْقُ رَبِّكَ خَيْرٌ وَأَبْقَى» .

Ṣāliḥ, the son of Imam Aḥmad ibn Ḥanbal, ℛ said: 'I said to my father: Aḥmad al-Dawraqī was given a thousand *Dinār*,' and so he said, 'O my beloved son, *and your Lord's provision is better, and more enduring*.[63]

وَقَالَ المَيْمُوْنِيُّ: «قَالَ أَحْمَدُ: رَأَيْتُ الخَلْوَةَ أَرْوَحَ لِقَلْبِي» .

Al-Maymūnī reported that Aḥmad Ibn Ḥanbal ℛ said: 'I found retreat [from people and especially those in power] to be more relaxing for my heart.'[64]

Aḥmad ibn Ḥanbal ℛ earned a meager income as a bread-seller and maintained a modest lifestyle throughout his life which enabled him to develop empathy and tenderness towards those in poverty like him. Incidently, his rejection of gifts and wealth earned him the respect of the upper class, 'be unattached to this world and Allah will love you; be unattached to what is in people's possession and people will love you' as the saying goes.

عن الـمَرُّوذيّ قَالَ: «لَمْ أَرَ الفَقِيرَ فِي مَجْلِسٍ أَعَزَّ مِنْهُ عِنْدَ أَبِي عَبْدِ اللهِ. كَانَ مَائِلًا إِلَيْهِمْ، مُقْصِرًا عَنْ أَهْلِ الدُّنْيَا. وَكَانَ فِيهِ حِلْمٌ، وَلَمْ يَكُنْ بِالعَجُولِ. وَكَانَ كَثِيرَ التَّوَاضُعِ، تَعْلُوهُ السَّكِينَةُ والوَقَارُ».

Al-Marrūdhī said: 'I have not seen a poor person more honoured in any assembly more than he was in the assembly of Imam Aḥmad ﷺ; he was always inclined towards the poor and neglectful of the people of this worldly life. He was forbearing and never hasty; He was also extremely humble, always marked by tranquility and gracefulness.'[65]

Wealth may hinder one from getting close to Allah. This is why some great men, such as al-Ḥasan al-Baṣrī ﷺ and Imam Aḥmad ﷺ, shunned this world and chose to live an ascetic life. But affluence can also be a means of serving one's community and Islam at large as was the case with Imam Mālik ﷺ and Imam Abū Ḥanīfah ﷺ. In any case, one should never feel inferior or superior to another person on account of one's wealth or his. Financial disparities, social classes and even race are things destined but they do not decide the superiority or inferiority of people. The great Muslim predecessors were more concerned with what mattered most, their *īmān* and closeness to Allah and His Messenger.

HIS DEATH

After the *miḥnah* or great trial, Imam Aḥmad ﵀ returned to his passion in life: teaching Hadith. He spend the remaining thirty-seven years of his life teaching the *Dīn* until his death at the age of 77 on Friday, the 12th of Rabīʿ al-Awwal of the year 241 AH/855 CE. When rebutting the Mu'tazilites, Imam Aḥmad ﵀ dismissed the crowds that were converging to accept their doctrines, remarking how funeral processions *(janā'iz)* shall be the criterion that decide who, of the two parties, was right and who was wrong.

أَحْمَد بن حَنْبَل يَقُولُ: «قُولُوا لِأَهْلِ البِدَعِ: بَيْنَنَا وَبَيْنَكُمْ الجَنَائِزَ».

It is reported that his *janāzah* was attended by 800,000 people,[66] one of the largest congregations of people witnessed at that time. From birth until death, Imam Aḥmad's ﵀ life was fraught with tests and difficulties but he was steadfast in the face of temptations and oppression. He left to posterity a tremendous legacy, acknowledged even by those who were not Muslim. His treatment of the poor and rejection of all the temptations of the royal court earned him the love of Christians, Jews, Zoroastrian and others, and his death affected many of them as well.

As the vicegerents of Allah on earth, our responsibilities and duties are not just confined to Muslims but also extend to all humanity. Despite his stern demeanour and strict approach in interpreting the Sunnah, Imam Aḥmad ibn Ḥanbal ﵀ was still able to positively affect people from all persuasions and walks of life. Oftentimes, Muslims use the excuse that non-Muslims do not like them because of what they wear or look like. The reality however is that kindness and compassion break all kinds of walls and bring different people together.

إمام البخاري

Imam al-Bukhārī

The Foremost Imam of Hadith

INTRODUCTION

IMAM AL-BUKHĀRĪ ﵀ was born on the 13th of Shawwāl of the year 194 AH/ 809 CE. His full name is Muhammad ibn Ismāʿīl ibn Ibrāhīm ibn al-Mughīrah al-Bukhārī. Bukhara, where he was born and to which he is attributed, did not produce any scholar of note before him; it was only after the emergence of Imam al-Bukhārī ﵀ that Bukhara, in modern Uzbekistan, became known in the whole Muslim world.

By the second century of the Hijrah deviant groups started to emerge in the lands of the caliphate, such as the *Khawārij* and the *Rawāfiḍ* who attacked and defamed the Companions of the Prophet ﷺ and their collective legacy. Through such attacks on the Prophetic Companions, they also disparaged most of the Hadith, since all the Prophetic sayings and statements were related via these same Prophetic Companions. Without the tremendous efforts, integrity and knowledge of the narrators of Hadith, the teachings of the Prophet ﷺ would have never reached us and the teachings of Islam would have been forgotten or lost. Imam al-Bukhārī ﵀ was a pillar in Hadith whose role in the preservation of the Prophetic traditions, and their passing down to future generations of Muslims, is immense. He is most renowned for his compilation of the most authentic Hadith collection, *Ṣaḥīḥ al-Bukhārī*, which is taught to students of Islamic sciences across the Muslim world. Imam al-Bukhārī's whole life was dedicated to disseminating the Prophetic Practice and Islamic knowledge.

THE PARENTS OF IMAM AL-BUKHĀRĪ

In the case of Imam al-Bukhārī, ﵀ his ascent to greatness and noble qualities started with his parents. His father was mentored by the eminent scholar ʿAbdullāh ibn al-Mubārak but he also studied under Ḥammād ibn Zayd ﵀ and Imam Mālik ibn Anas. ﵀ Thus, his father was a great scholar of Hadith in his own right.

Shortly after Imam al-Bukhārī's ﵀ birth, his father passed away and his mother took on the responsibility of raising her family. During his infancy, Imam al-Bukhārī ﵀ had weak eyesight that deteriorated into complete blindness. In desperation, his mother made sincere and constant supplications for him which lasted two to three years. One night, Imam al-Bukhārī's ﵀ mother received in a dream the glad tidings she was longing for from the

Prophet Ibrāhīm ♦ who told her that Allah had restored Imam al-Bukhārī's ♦ eyesight thanks to her continuous supplications.[67] Indeed, his eyesight was not only restored but became stronger and better than it had been before he completely lost it thanks to the sincere prayers of his mother. It is reported that Imam al-Bukhārī ♦ wrote at night without using a candle, needing only the light of the moon. As a way of showing gratitude to Allah for His immense favour, his mother had the young Bukhārī memorise the Holy Qur'an by the age of six. And on the instruction and encouragement of his mother, he began attending the assemblies of Hadith.

Muslims must show a great deal of respect and express sincere thanks to the anonymous Muslim women and mothers who contributed to the *Dīn* and are often unacknowledged and not given enough credit for their efforts. The immensity of Islamic scholarship is not just due to the scholars themselves, but also to those who have mentored them and helped them to follow the way of sacred knowledge.

HIS TRAVELS

Imam al-Bukhārī ♦ completed his studies in Bukhara and, at the age of 16, travelled to perform the *Ḥajj* with his mother and older brother. The journey to *Ḥajj* was streneous as they often ran out of provision. After performing the obligation of *Ḥajj*, he took permission from his mother to remain in the Hejaz, the western coastal region of the Arabian Peninsula which includes the Holy cities of Makkah and Madinah. The Imam only opted to remain in the Hejaz to seek more knowledge as he learnt all there was to learn in his native country.

At the age of eighteen, Imam al-Bukhārī ﷺ wrote two texts next to the tomb of the Prophet Muhammad ﷺ. One of these is his *al-Tārīkh al-Kabīr* which dealt with the biographies of Hadith narrators.

سَمِعْتُ عَبْدَ القُدّوسِ بنَ هَمَّامٍ يَقُوْلُ: «سَمِعْتُ عِدَّةً مِنَ المَشَايِخِ، يَقُوْلُوْنَ: حَوَّلَ مُحَمَّدُ بنُ إِسْمَاعِيْلَ تَرَاجِمَ جَامِعِهِ بَيْنَ قَبْرِ رَسُوْلِ اللهِ ﷺ وَمِنْبَرِهِ، وَكَانَ يُصَلِّي لِكُلِّ تَرْجَمَةٍ رَكْعَتَيْنِ».

ʿAbd al-Qudūs ibn Hammām said: 'I heard many teachers say: "Imam al-Bukhārī ﷺ wrote the biographies of the narrators of his *al-Jāmiʿ al-Ṣaḥīḥ* while sitting between the tomb and *minbar* of the Prophet ﷺ . He used to offer two units of prayers for each biography he wrote.'[68]

The other text is *Qaḍāyā al-Ṣaḥābah wa'l-Tābiʿīn*. In this work, al-Bukhārī ﷺ praised the Companions of the Prophet ﷺ and affirmed their trustworthiness and knowledge at a time when some deviant factions were becoming increasingly derogatory towards the *Ṣaḥābah*. Imam al-Bukhārī ﷺ later travelled outside the Hejaz to seek more sacred knowledge. After tremendous efforts and uncessing travelling, he collected Prophetic narrations from over one thousand scholars. His travelling after the Hejaz took to Baghdad which became the centre of Hadith studies after the death of Imam Mālik ﷺ and his student Imam al-Shāfiʿī. ﷺ In Baghdad, he met great scholars such as Isḥāq ibn Rahwayh ﷺ and Imam Aḥmad ibn Ḥanbal r. But not only did he learn and memorise thousands of Prophetic traditions, he also appropriated their noble character traits and embodied them in his own life. This is the real way that Hadith is truly memorized and preserved, not by merely writing it down or solely commiting it to memory. After seeking knowledge for an additional sixteen years, Imam al-Bukhārī ﷺ had transmitted Prophetic narrations from over 80,000 narrators. He was an exceptional student who approached learning in ways that were unheard of. A conversation between his students highlights well how exceptional these ways were.

وَقَالَ مُحَمَّدُ بنُ أَبِي حَاتِمِ الْوَرَّاقُ: «سَمِعْتُ حَاشِدَ بنَ إِسْمَاعِيْلَ وَآخَرَ يَقُولَانِ: «كَانَ أَبُو عَبْدِ اللهِ الْبُخَارِيُّ يَخْتَلِفُ مَعَنَا إِلَى مَشَايِخِ الْبَصْرَةِ، وَهُوَ غُلَامٌ فَلَا يَكْتُبُ حَتَّى أَتَى عَلَى ذَلِكَ أَيَّامٍ فَكُنَّا نَقُولُ لَهُ: «إِنَّكَ تَخْتَلِفُ مَعَنَا ولَا تَكْتُبُ فَمَ تَصْنَعُ؟». فَقَالَ لَنَا يَوْماً بَعْدَ سِتَّةَ عَشَرَ يَوْماً: «إِنَّكَمَا قَدْ أَكْثَرْتُمَا عَلَيَّ وَأَلْحَحْتُمَا فَاعْرِضَا عَلَيَّ مَا كَتَبْتُمَا» فَأَخْرَجْنَا إِلَيْهِ مَا كَانَ عِنْدَنَا فَزَادَ عَلَى خَمْسَةَ عَشَرَ أَلْفِ حَدِيثٍ فَقَرَأَهَا كُلَّهَا عَنْ ظَهْرِ الْقَلْبِ حَتَّى جَعَلَنَا نُحْكِمُ كُتُبَنَا مِنْ حِفْظِهِ، ثُمَّ قَالَ: «أَتَرَوْنَ أَنِّي أَخْتَلِفُ هَدَراً وَأُضَيِّعُ أَيَّامِي؟». فَعَرَفْنَا أَنَّهُ لَا يَتَقَدَّمُهُ أَحَدٌ».

Ḥāshid ibn Ismāʿīl and two others said: 'Abū ʿAbdullāh al-Bukhārī ﵀ used to attend along with us the study circles of the scholars of Basra when he was a young lad, but he never wrote down anything. This carried on for several days until we said to him: "You come with us and yet you do not write down anything, so what are you up to?" One day, after sixteen days of him not writing down anything he heard from his teachers, he said: "You have pestered me and insisted on wanting to know what I was up to, so show me what you have written down." So we showed him what we had written down which was more than fifteen thousand Prophetic narrations. Then, he read all these narration from memory to the point that we started correcting what we wrote on the basis of what he memorised. Then he said: "Do you still think that I just waste my time and only squander my days?"'[68]

HIS CHARACTER TRAITS

Imam al-Bukhāri ﵀ was renowned particularly for his legendary memory, the dignity and integrity he displayed throughout his life out of deference to his position as a *muḥaddith*, or Hadith scholar, and his stringent and rigorous approach in accepting the narrations of the Messenger of Allah ﷺ. From an early age, he had a remarkable ability for memorization. A conversation he had with

Aḥmad ibn Ḥafṣ captures well this tremendous gift for memorisation. Imam al-Dakhīlī ﵏ was a *muḥaddith* in Bukhara. One day he related in his circle a chain of transmission (*sanad*) but Imam al-Bukhārī ﵏, who was then eleven years old, raised an objection regarding it. Imam al-Dakhīlī ﵏ was unhappy that a young boy was telling him he had made an mistake. After checking that chain of transmission against what he had committed to writing, he realised that he had indeed made a mistake. On the request of Imam al-Dakhīlī ﵏, Imam al-Bukhārī ﵏ read the correct chain of transmission as Imam al-Dakhīlī ﵏ had written. So impressed with him, Imam al-Dakhīlī ﵏ remarked that the young man was going to have a special status with Allah. Imam al-Bukhārī ﵏ never gave up his study of Hadith and continued to commit himself to the collection and memorizing of Prophetic narrations throughout his entire life, as the following interaction shows:

وَقَالَ أَبُو جَعْفَرٍ مُحَمَّدُ بنُ أَبِي حَاتِمٍ: «قُلْتُ لأَبِي عَبْدِ اللهِ: تَحْفَظُ جَمِيْعَ مَا أَدْخَلْتَ فِي المُصَنَّفِ؟» فَقَالَ: «لاَ يَخفى عليَّ جَمِيْعُ مَا فِيْهِ».

Muhammad ibn Abī Ḥātim said to Imam al-Bukhārī ﵏: 'Have you memorised everything you have put in your work?' Al-Bukhārī ﵏ replied: 'There is nothing in it that I have not memorised.'[70]

In another famous episode, the scholars of Baghdad wanted to test the legendary memory of Imam al-Bukhārī ﵏

in public. Ten scholars read to him ten different Prophetic narrations with their respective chains of transmission. However, these chains were intentionally changed to confuse him. After reading to him all the hundred narrations, Imam al-Bukhārī ﵀ repeated from memory all these narrations with their correct chains of transmission.[71]

Imam al-Bukhārī ﵀ was aware of the importance of leading a dignified and upright life, being entrusted as he was to narrate Hadith and preserve it to posterity. On one of his trips by sea, a fellow passenger began to converse with him and eventually asked for some money from the Imam's personal purse which contained one thousand silver coins. The Imam obliged. Later on, the same traveler caused an uproar on the ship, claiming that someone stole his money, a scheme he devised to get hold of the Imam's personal purse. Understanding what was going on, Imam al-Bukhārī ﵀ threw the purse into the ocean. After an elongated search, the boat officials became upset with the traveler's false allegation. When this traveler directly approached the Imam and unashamedly asked him about the whereabout of his purse's location, Imam al-Bukhārī ﵀ informed him that he threw it overboard, saying:

«يَا جَاهِلُ ...أَتدرِي أَنَّنِي أفنَيْتُ حَياتِي كُلَّهَا فِي جَمْعِ حَدِيثِ رَسُولِ اللهِ ﷺ وعَرَفَنِي العَالَمُ وَوَثّقُوا فِيَّ وَصَدَّقُونِي فِي كُلِّ مَا أَرْوِيهِ مِنْ أَحَـادِيثٍ شَـرِيفَـةٍ ، فَكَيْفَ يَنْبَغِي لِي أَنْ أَجْعَلَ نَفْسِي عُرْضَةً للتُهْمَةِ مِنْ أَجْلِ دَرَاهِمَ مَعْدُودَةٍ».

‘O ignorant man! Don’t you know that I have spent my life collecting the Hadith of the Prophet ﷺ, and the world has come to know and trust and believe in me? So how should I expose myself to accusations on my character for the sake of a few silver coins?’

ṢAḤĪḤ AL-BUKHĀRĪ

There are conflicting numbers regarding the number of Prophetic traditions that Imam al-Bukhārī ﵀ had committed to memory, although it is fairly certain he had memorized at least 600,000 Prophetic narrations. It was while he was in the circle of Imam Isḥāq ibn Rahwayh ﵀ that Imam al-Bukhārī ﵀ was inspired to compile the now famous *Ṣaḥīḥ al-Bukhārī*.

قَالَ البُخَارِيُّ: «كُنْتُ عِنْدَ إِسْحَاقَ بْنِ رَاهْوَيْه فَقَالَ بَعْضُ أَصْحَابِنَا: «لَوْ جَمَعْتُم كِتَاباً مُخْتَصَرًا لِسُنَنِ النَّبِيِّ ﷺ» فَوَقَعَ ذَلِكَ فِي قَلْبِي، فَأَخَذْتُ فِي جَمْعِ هَذَا الكِتَابِ».

Imam al-Bukhārī ﵀ said: ‘I was one day sitting in the assembly of Isḥāq Ibn Rahwayh ﵀, and one of our fellow companions said: “If only you would compile a concise book containing the narrations of the Prophet ﷺ.” So I liked the idea and started compiling this book.’[72]

The full title of *Ṣaḥīḥ al-Bukhārī* is *al-Jāmiʿ al-Ṣaḥīḥ al-Musnad al-Mukhtaṣar min Ḥadīth Rasūl Allāh wa-Sunanih wa-Ayyāmih* [The Concise Abridged Compendium of the Hadiths of the Messenger of Allah that Have Contiguous Chains of Transmission, his Practices and Momentous Events]. Out of six-hundred thousand known hadith, one hundred thousand of which Imam al-Bukhārī ﵀ had confirmed as authentic according to the rules he laid out for the authentification of Prophetic narrations, he included 7,275 Prophetic narrations in this collection. Before including any Prophetic narration in his collection, Imam al-Bukhārī ﵀ performed major ritual ablution (*ghusl*) and performed two units of prayer.[73]

قال الإِمَامُ البُخَـــارِيُّ: «مَـــا وَضَعْتُ فِي كِتَابِي (الصَّحِيح) حَديثًا إِلَّا اِغْتَسَلْتُ قَبْلَ ذَلِكَ وَصَلَّيْتُ رَكْعَتَيْنِ».

The compilation of the *Ṣaḥīḥ* which took over sixteen years to complete was highly praised by the greatest scholars of Hadith including Imam Aḥmad ibn Ḥanbal ﵀, ʿAlī ibn al-Madīnī ﵀ and Yaḥya ibn Maʿīn ﵀ . In fact, *Ṣaḥīḥ al-Bukhārī* is considered the most authentic text of Islam after the Qur'an.

ونَقَلَ عَبْدُ الرَّحْمَن بْن رَسَاين أَنَّهُ قَالَ: سَمِعْتُ البُخَارِيَّ يَقُوْلُ: «صَـنَّفْتُ (الصَّحِيْحَ) فِي سِتَّ عَشْرَةَ سَنَـةً، وَجَـعَلْتُـهُ حُجَّـةً فِيْمَـا بَيْنِي وَبَيْنَ اللهِ تَعَالَى».

> 'Abd al-Raḥmān ibn Rasāyan reported that he
> heard al-Bukhārī ◈ say: 'I authored the *Ṣaḥīḥ*
> over a period of sixteen years and I made it as a
> proof between me and Allah Most High.'[74]

The science of Hadith is thorough and contextualized. It takes long years and tremendous efforts to familiarise oneself with its different branches; in fact, its study nowadays is a lifetime commitment. It is worth emphasizing that scholarship requires far more than an online search-engine, and for those committed to speak only with knowledge, they must be serious about it and formally study it with qualified scholars.

LATER YEARS AND DEATH

In 250 AH, Imam al-Bukhārī ◈ moved to Nishapur in Central Asia. There he attracted thousands of students, including one who would eventually be known as one of the most famous scholars of Hadith, Imam Muslim ibn al-Ḥajjāj ◈. Some of the Scholars in Nishapur were upset that their students abandoned their assemblies to join the study circle of Imam al-Bukhārī. ◈ In order to discredit him, some spread rumours that Imam al-Bukhārī ◈ moved to Nishapur to spread heretical views. These rumours forced Imam al-Bukhārī ◈ to leave Nishapur and return to his home city of Bukhara. In Bukhara, he was pressured by the governor to give private lessons to his children but he refused and explained to him that his lessons are open to all students from every walk of life. His stay in Bukhara did not last long and he was forced to leave his home city as a result of the envy and scheming of unscrupulous people. Finally, he settled in Kharteng, a village on the outskirts of Samarqand.

As one can see, reformers and society-builders may have to deal with boycot, poverty, persecution and political pressure. But this should not come as a surprise to anyone, as the ones who are more severely tested are the Prophets and then those who come close to follow their example. The challenges and trials one faces in life are commensurate with the degree of one's closeness to Allah.

In Kharteng, Imam al-Bukhārī ﵀ made the following powerful *du'ā*:

«اللَّهُمَّ إِنَّهُ قَدْ ضَاقَتْ عَلَيَّ الأَرْضُ بِمَا رَحُبَتْ فَاقْبِضْنِي إِلَيْكَ».

'O Allah !The earth has become too narrow for me despite its vastness, so take me back to You.'[75]

After spending his entire life in the service of the *Dīn* and the Muslim Ummah, he had enough of this *Dunyā* and wanted to be with his Lord. On the first night of Shawwāl in 256 AH/870 CE, Imam al-Bukhārī ﵀ fell ill and passed away in the village of Kharteng. Multiple sources report that Imam al-Bukhārī ﵀ was seen in a dream after his death. In the dream, the Prophetic Companions found the Prophet ﷺ waiting and so they asked him: 'Who are you waiting for?' He responded,

'I am waiting for Imam al-Bukhārī. ﷺ' Though Imam al-Bukhārī ﷺ never physically fought in any battles, he was a soldier who fought to preserve the Sunnah of the Prophet ﷺ. Not only did he protect the knowledge through which our Creator is known via His Messenger ﷺ, but he also laid out solid foundations and rules for the integrity of the science of Hadith. May Imam al-Bukhārī ﷺ be an inspiration to all Muslims such that they familiarise themselves with the Prophet ﷺ also, in order to find peace and contentment in their lives.

صلاح الدين
الأيوبي

Ṣalāḥ al-Dīn al-Ayyūbī

The Great Liberator

EARLY LIFE

YŪSUF IBN Ayyūb, more commonly known as Ṣalāḥ al-Dīn al-Ayyūbī ﵀ was born in 532 AH/1137 CE in the city of Tikrit, Iraq. This city was conquered by the Muslims in 16 AH/637 CE during the reign of ʿUmar ibn al-Khaṭṭāb ﵁. Shortly after the birth of Ṣalāḥ al-Dīn, and on the invitation of Mosul's governor, ʿImād al-Dīn Zangī, Najm al-Dīn Ayyūb, Ṣalāḥ al-Dīn's father, his paternal uncle Asad al-Dīn Shīrkūh and their families left Tikrit and moved to Mosul. Imād al-Dīn Zangī was a Turkic nobleman who seized power over both Mosul and Aleppo when still quite young in age. Zangī gradually consolidated his power in Syria and Iraq after a civil war between different heirs within the Seljuk dynasty. He went on to capture the fortress of Edessa, one of the Crusaders' bases from which numerous incursions were made into Muslim lands. The cities of Baalbak (in modern day Lebanon) and

Damascus were both occupied by the Zangids. Najm al-Dīn was appointed as governor of Baalbak, which meant that Ṣalāḥ al-Dīn spent the earlier part of his childhood there. In Baalbak, he studied Islamic knowledge and the art of war.[76] In later childhood, he lived in Syria where he grew to appreciate and understand the different political and social trends in Muslim lands, which were dominated by the conflict with the Crusaders. Ṣalāḥ al-Dīn had a keen interest in Islamic studies. According to ʿAli M. al-Ṣallābī, 'he [Ṣalāḥ al-Dīn] memorized the Qur'an, studied *fiqh* and Hadith under some of the leading scholars of Syria and Mesopotamia.'[77] In the process of discussing Ṣalāḥ al-Dīn's interests in Islamic studies, the British Orientalist Stanley Lane-Poole wrote:

> His literary tastes tended to the theological, he loved poetry indeed, but he less than keen on dialectic, and to hear holy traditions traced and verified, canon law formulated, passages in the Koran explained, and sound orthodoxy vindicated, inspired him with a strange delight.[78]

In 546 AH/1150 CE, Ṣalāḥ al-Dīn ﵀ served his paternal uncle Asad al-Dīn Shīrkūh who was a strong ally of Nūr al-Dīn, the sultan of the Zangids at the time. Nūr ad-Dīn took a special interest in Ṣalāḥ al-Dīn due to his intellect and wisdom. Ṣalāh al-Dīn served as Nūr al-Dīn's private secretary and then as a liaison officer between Nūr al-Dīn and his senior commanders such as his uncle.[79] During that time, Ṣalāḥ al-Dīn benefited from the company of his mentors such as his father, his uncle, and Nūr al-Dīn. Nūr al-Dīn was eager to implement the most pristine form of the *Sharīʿah* and abolish all the wayward customs and traditions prevalent in Egypt and Syria. He was a pious and godfearing individual who devoted his nights to prayer and promoted Islamic scholarship in the lands he controlled. He was a man of unflinching faith, confident in his extensive preparations, yet always turning to Allah for success and victory on the battlefield. When not on the battlefield, he was generous to the poor and the needy. In one instance, his advisors suggested that funds earmarked for charity should be put to better use if diverted to the war effort. To this, Nūr al-Dīn responded, 'The poor have a right to benefit from public revenues and so how can I ask them to forgo what is due to them?'[80] Ṣalāḥ al-Dīn ﷺ excelled in the favourable environment he lived in under the tutelage of accomplished and sincere leaders. He was even appointed chief of police in Damascus by Nūr al-Dīn which gave him the opportunity to eradicate major crimes in the city.[81] The extensive experience that Ṣalāḥ al-Dīn gained while working under his mentors prepared him well for his future role as an Ayyubid sultan.

CAMPAIGN IN EGYPT

Nūr al-Dīn ordered Ṣalāḥ ad-Dīn al-Ayyūbi ﷺ and his uncle to conduct a military campaign to Egypt. According to a counselor of Ṣalāḥ al-Dīn, *Qāḍī* Bahā' al-Dīn ibn Shaddād, the former felt that he was dragged against his will when ordered to join this campaign. He thought he might be killed in the process when all he wanted to do was pursuing sacred knowledge.[82] At the time, Egypt was the scene of tumultuous political events involving the Crusaders, the Fatimids, different Muslim factions and the Zangi dynasty, all of whom were vying for the control of this Muslim land. News reached Nūr al-Dīn that King Amalric and his Crusading army had attacked Egypt with the support of some Fatimid generals. He therefore dispatched Asad al-Dīn Shīrkūh and Ṣalāḥ al-Dīn al-Ayyūbī ﵀ to give support to al-Sa'dī against the Crusaders and the Fatimid generals who helped them. Asad al-Dīn defeated the rogue Fatimid generals and handed power to al-Sa'dī. Shāwir ibn Mujāwir al-Sa'dī, one of the governors of Upper West Egypt, then betrayed Nūr al-Dīn's men and allied himself with King Amalric. Asad al-Dīn and Ṣalāḥ al-Dīn ﵀ were forced to cut their losses and retreat. They returned to Egypt again in 562 AH/1166 CE and in 563 AH/1167 CE, they waged a war against the Crusaders while Asad al-Dīn and Ṣalāḥ al-Dīn pressed on into Alexandria.

After the conquest of Alexandria, Ṣalāḥ al-Dīn was appointed its governor and was in action again soon after that as he resisted a siege by the Crusader and Byzantine troops. Eventually, an agreement was reached by both sides to withdraw from Egypt. The truce was broken by the Crusaders either because King Amalric sought to occupy Egypt after the Syrian troops withdrew from it or because Amalric heard that al-Sa'dī was looking to re-ally himself with the Syrian troops. For a third time, Asad al-Dīn Shīrkūh and Ṣalāḥ al-Dīn entered Egypt, upon which the Crusaders retreated without putting a fight.[83]

Ṣalāḥ al-Dīn al-Ayyūbi ﷺ was then appointed the Chief Minister (*vizir*) in the Fatimid Caliphate. After gaining the upper hand in Egypt, Ibn Shaddād described how Ṣalāḥ al-Dīn made a new resolve and became a changed man:

> The world and its pleasures lost all significance in his eyes. With a heartfelt sense of gratitude for the favour bestowed by God on him he gave up drinking, renounced the temptations of pleasure, and took to the life of sweat and toil which went on increasing with the passage of time.[84]

He maintained good relations with Nūr al-Dīn and after the death of the Fatimid Caliph al-'Aḍid, Ṣalāḥ al-Dīn ﷺ reintegrated Egypt in the Abbasid Caliphate. He led the province of Egypt under the leadership of Nūr al-Dīn who passed away in 569 AH/1174 CE. His eleven-year old son al-Malik al-Ṣālih Ismā'īl became the new sultan. Divisions flared amongst the Caliphate's leadership, between the young sultan's guardians and other princes. These princes played politics with each other and, in order to have an edge over their adversaries, made treaties with the Crusaders. Eventually, the people of Damascus invited Ṣalāḥ al-Dīn to lead the nation.

When Ṣalāḥ al-Dīn became aware of the support of the people, he traveled to Damascus and dealt with the political intrigues happening there while safeguarding the position of the young al-Malik al-Ṣāliḥ as sultan. Disturbed by the internal political turmoil and disunity plaguing the Sultanate, he set out on a mission to unite the neighbouring Muslim lands, thus conquering Homs, Hama, al-Maʿarrah, Manbaj, ʿAzaz and other localities. When he then returned to Egypt, he was informed of the death of al-Ṣāliḥ. After capturing Aleppo from al-Ṣaliḥ's successor in 579 AH/1182 CE, Ṣalāḥ al-Dīn al-Ayyūbī ﵀ went on to unify all the Muslim mini-states with the view of ending internal conflict and strengthening the Sultanate against the threat of the Crusaders. This marked the beginning of the Ayyubid Empire. Using effective military strategy as well as diplomacy, Ṣalāḥ al-Dīn ﵀ sent his army to end the civil war between Muslims in Yemen and proceeded to establish control over that land. He then captured Tripoli, Narqah, and the eastern part of Tunisia to Qabis.[85] By the time of his death, his sultanate controlled the Hejaz, Yemen, the Levant, Iraq, Egypt and approximately half of Africa's northern coast.

While renowned for his conquest of Jerusalem, most of Ṣalāḥ al-Dīn's ﵀ life and efforts were devoted to unifying Muslims lands. His greater goal was to allow the Muslims to build a solid and united front capable of facing the threat of the Crusaders. That is probably why his kingdom did not last very long after him but Jerusalem did.

THE CRUSADERS

The main threat to the Muslims in the time of Ṣalāḥ al-Dīn ﷺ were the Christian European Crusades. Several factors contributed in launching these crusades to capture the Holy Land. First, it was a means to unify an infighting Europe against a single threat. Second, the recapture of what they considered holy sites, including the birthplace of Jesus Christ, would have constituted a victory for the religious authority of Europe. Third, crushing the Islamic empire, which was a constant threat at the borders of the Byzantine Empire, would have been a tremendous strategic victory. Europe detected weakness in the world of Islam due to the infighting between Muslim rulers who controlled diifferent parts of vast, disunited Muslim territories. Some Muslim rulers even turned to Europe for assistance to defeat their rivals. The first crusade was in 490 AH/1096 CE, almost forty years before the birth of Ṣalāḥ al-Dīn al-Ayyūbī ﷺ. The Crusaders swiftly captured greater Palestine and the coast of the Levant.

Then they captured the city of Jerusalem in 493 AH/1099 CE and put its local population to the sword. A first-hand account of the aftermath of the event describes it as follows:

> So terrible, it is said, was the carnage which followed, that the horses of the crusaders who rode up to the mosque of Omar were knee-deep in the stream of blood. Infants were seized

> from their feet and dashed against the walls or whirled over the battlements, while Jews were all burnt alive in the synagogue... a massacre followed in which the bodies of men, women and children were hacked and hewn until their fragments lay tossed together in heaps. The work of slaughter ended, the streets of the city were washed by Saracen prisoners.[86]

It is estimated that seventy thousand Muslims were killed when Jerusalem first fell into the hands of the Crusaders. Rivalry between Muslim leaders elicited the invasion of the Holy lands by the Crusaders. Thus, internal strife indicates that weakness is often self-inflicted. This is not dissimilar to the state of Muslims today. When Muslims were able to unite, they were able to recapture the third holiest site of Islam. If Muslims wish to strengthen themselves against exploitation, then Muslim leaders, whether in small communities or large countries, must learn to set aside their internal squabbles.

After gaining control over Greater Egypt and Syria, Ṣalāḥ al-Dīn ﷺ prepared his armies to expel the Crusaders from the Holy lands. He just waited for the opportune moment to do so. This came thanks to the wanton behaviour and recklessness of one of Islam's bitter enemies, Reginald of Châtillon. The latter, a crusader from Europe, married Constance, a princess from a crusader state then called Antioch.[87] Reginald was a 'cruel and violent' prince who fought against the Byzantines and Muslims. He was captured by the Muslim governor of Aleppo in 556/557 AH 1160/1161 CE and released fifteen years later. He then travelled to Jerusalem and married Stephanie of Milly which allowed him to take control of the Kerak region in western Jordan, a region frequented by Muslim caravans. In Kerak, Reginald violated a truce he signed with Ṣalāḥ al-Dīn ﷺ when he attacked and plundered a Muslim caravan travelling through the area. In this attack, he mocked the Muslims by telling them to ask the Prophet ﷺ to come for their help and massacred most of those who travelled with the caravan. Reginald also attempted to attack the city of Makkah and threatened to move the grave of the Prophet ﷺ. Ṣalāḥ al-Dīn ﷺ used this opportunity and rallied his troops to recapture Jerusalem.

Throughout the Crusades, the Muslims were generally on the defense against Christian European incursions. Just as with the Conquest of Makkah, the Conquest of Jerusalem was triggered by Reginald's violation of the treaty he signed with Muslims. Islam teaches Muslims to not initiate agitations or attack others unless they are wronged.

THE BATTLE OF ḤAṬṬĪN AND THE CONQUEST OF JERUSALEM

The Battle of Ḥaṭṭīn and the subsequent conquest of Jerusalem is one of the greatest victories of Muslims over their enemies. Ṣalāḥ al-Dīn ﷺ sent his advisers around his territory and eventually rallied troops consisting of 20,000 to 30,000 soldiers. The Muslim army began by besieging a Crusader town called Tiberias and settled there and secured the nearby lake for the supply of water. The Crusaders responded by sending an army of their own and attempted to settle by the Springs of Ḥaṭṭin but the Muslim army blocked their access to the sources of water in the area. The hot weather took its toll on the crusading army. When the Crusaders made camp, the Muslim army surrounded it and sent volleys of arrows on it, setting fire to the dry grass. Ṣalāḥ al-Dīn's ﷺ army easily defeated the Crusaderers and the King of Jerusalem, Guy of Lusignan, along with Reginald of Châtillon, Humphrey IV of Toron and other high ranking Crusaders were taken captive. Due to the egrigousness of his crimes against innocent Muslim pilgrims, Ṣalāḥ al-Dīn personally executed the murderous Reginald of Châtillon while almost all the other prisoners were pardoned and eventually released. With the depletion of the Crusading forces in Jerusalem and its neighbouring regions, the victory at Ḥaṭṭin made way for a straight shot toward Jerusalem.

Ṣalāḥ al-Dīn al-Ayyūbī ﷺ besieged Jerusalem in order to get the Crusaders out of it instead of trying to invade it. He sent an envoy to the Crusaders asking them to surrender for the sake of the safeguard of the holy places and the safety of the civilians in the city. The Crusaders refused to surrender, leaving Ṣalāḥ al-Dīn ﷺ no choice but to attack them. A week later, the Crusaders surrendered on the proviso that they would leave Jerusalem within forty days and pay a ransom of ten gold pieces for each one of their men, five for each of their women and two for each of their boys. The tables had now turned on the crusaders and Ṣalāḥ al-Dīn could have opted to massacre them as they did to the Muslim and Jewish inhabitants of Jerusalem when they conquered it for the first time.

However, Ṣalāḥ al-Dīn al-Ayyūbī ﵀ demonstrated the highest degrees of restraint and forgave them. Has any world leader whose people had endured so much at the hand of their enemies shown Ṣalāḥ al-Dīn's ﵀ level of compassion and chivalery towards their enemies? Not only did he forgive his enemies, but he also helped the elderly who left the city by providing them with money and mounts to ride and carry their belongings. He also allowed prisoners to be reunited with their families. The elderly, the disabled, the poor and the clerics were allowed to leave Jerusalem in peace without paying any ransom. Muslims purchased the items that those leaving the city could not carry with them. Eventually, many were permitted to leave Jerusalem without paying any ransom.[88] The stark contrast in the treatment of the Muslims and Jews in the first Crusade and that of the Christians after the Muslim conquest of Jerusalem illustrates the tolerance of Islam and its presumptive justice that supercedes revenge and anger. It was a tremendous victory for Ṣalāḥ al-Dīn ﵀ and the Muslim Ummah. It is noteworthy that the conquest of Jerusalem happened on a Friday, the 27th of Rajab 583 AH/1183 CE, on the same day that the Prophet ﷺ led all the prophets in prayer before he ascended to heaven. Ibn Shaddād said:

'It was the victory of victories...The joyful shouts of 'Allah is Great', and 'There is no god but Allah' rent the skies. After ninety years Friday prayer was again held in Jerusalem.'[89]

Ṣalāḥ al-Dīn al-Ayyūbī's ﷺ triumph and his success in unifying the Muslims triggered another Christian crusade. One of the leaders of this crusade was Richard I of England, more commonly known as Richard the Lionheart. Appointed at a young age as Duke of Normandy, he showed military and political prowess which prepared him for the Third Crusade. Upon hearing that Jerusalem had fallen to Ṣalāḥ al-Dīn's ﷺ army, he joined the Third Crusade and battled with the latter over the course of a year. Richard continuously tried to break Ṣalāḥ al-Dīn's ﷺ defences to make way for another siege of Jerusalem. Finally, Richard was able to defeat Ṣalāḥ al-Dīn's army at the Battle of Arsuf in 588 AH/1191 CE. The Muslim army faced Lionheart's army again at the Battle of Jaffa which ended by agreeing a three-year truce period whereby the Muslims retain Jerusalem and the Christian settlers were allowed to visit the city.

HIS CHARACTER TRAITS

Leaders and generals are typically remembered for their political and military prowess and Ṣalāḥ al-Dīn ﷺ is no exception in this regard. However, Ṣalāḥ al-Dīn ﷺ was more than a shrewed political leader and brilliant military strategist. Historical records have highlighted his remarkable generosity and unworldliness even when he was at the height of his power. Indeed, it is rare to find world leaders who are able to lead their nations and peoples while maintaining their devotion to Allah and remain pious and upright. Ṣalāḥ al-Dīn al-Ayyūbī ﵀ was undoubtedly one of these rare individuals and one of Islam's greatest sons.

Ṣalāḥ al-Dīn ﵀ showcased the importance of adhering to the tenets of Islam and his determination in this regard was highlighted by Ibn Shaddād who wrote:

> He was a regular in the performance of religious observances. Once he told me, 'I have not performed a single congregational prayer alone for the past several years.' Even during his illness, he would send for the Imam and force himself to perform the prayer behind him... He always kept the fast during the month of Ramadan... He delighted in hearing the Qur'an recited to him and it was not unoften that he listened to three or four chapters of the Holy Scripture from the battlement guards whom he sometimes visited during the night. He listened to the Qur'an with all his heart and soul until tears trickled down his cheeks...The Sultan had an unflinching trust and confidence in the beneficence of Allah. He used to turn with his heart and soul towards God in the moments of difficulty.[90]

During his last years, he struggled with fasting due to succumbing to one illness after another. Yet, he would have scribes note the days he missed so he could make up the fast at the earliest opportunity. He encouraged those around him to sit in the presence of scholars, especially those narrating the hadith of the Prophet ﷺ. He wept out of love for Islam and felt honoured that Allah ﷻ had allowed him to unify the Ummah of the Prophet ﷺ.

HIS DEATH

In 589 AH/1192 CE, Ṣalāḥ al-Dīn al-Ayyūbī رحمه الله became ill and seriously weak. Ibn Shaddād narrated that the sultan had one of his shaykhs recite the Holy Qur'an next to him as he lay semi-conscious. When the reciter got to the verse, *He is Allah; there is no god but He. He is the knower of the Unseen and the Visible; He is the All-merciful, the All-compassionate* from Surah *al-Ḥashr*, Ṣalāḥ al-Dīn al-Ayyūbī opened his eyes and said, 'Verily, this is correct,' and then passed away. This happened on Wednesday, the 27th of Safar 589 AH/1192 CE when Ṣalāḥ al-Dīn رحمه الله was fifty-five years old.[91] This sultan who reigned over a vast Muslim empire astoundingly left behind only one gold piece and forty-seven silver pieces as most of his wealth was given to the poor.

«وَكَرَمُهُ قَدَّسَ اللهُ رُوحَهُ كَانَ أَظْهَرَ مِنْ أَنْ يُسَطَّرَ وَأَشْهَرَ مِنْ أَنْ
يُذْكَرَ، لَكِنْ نَبَّهْتُ عَلَيْهِ جُمْلَةً، وَذَلِكَ أَنَّهُ مَلَكَ مَا مَلَكَ وَمَاتَ

وَلَمْ يُوجَدْ فِي خِزَانَتِهِ مِنَ الفِضَّةِ إِلَّا سَبْعَةٌ وَأَرْبَعُونَ دِرْهَمًا نَاصِرِيَّةٌ
وَمِنَ الذَّهَبِ إِلَّا جِرْمٌ وَاحِدٌ صُورِيٌّ مَا عَلِمْتُ وَزْنَهُ».

His generosity, may Allah bless his soul, was too much to write down, and so well known it doesn't need to be mentioned, but a testimony of this generosity was that he was the king of his massive kingdom, and he died with nothing in his possession except forty-seven dirhams, and a small amount of gold which I have not come across its weight.[92]

Power is not always the means through which change is effected. Muslim rulers at the time of Ṣalāḥ al-Dīn ﵀ had power but opted to keep feuds with one another at the expense of Islam's interests. One may ask: who in our time will, like Ṣalāḥ al-Dīn ﵀, change the lot of Islam and Muslims? How do Muslims garner socio-political influence like he did to improve their condition? In order for Muslims to change their lot, they must first relearn what it means to be Muslim, through serious and diligent study.

امام النووي

Imam al-Nawawī

The Role Model for Scholars

EARLY LIFE

ABŪ ZAKARIYYĀ Yaḥya ibn Sharaf al-Nawawī, more commonly known as Imam al-Nawawī ﷺ, was born in 631 AH/1230 CE in the town of Nawā, Syria. Unlike many notable scholars of Islam, he did not hail from a distinguished family known for its scholarly achievements or interest in sacred knowledge. But if he did not hail from a family known for its scholarly achievements, godfearingness and piety was not absent from it. Some accounts mention that Imam al-Nawawī's father, a seller of vegetables, avoided *ḥarām* earning and made sure his children consumed only what is *ḥalāl*.

As a young child, Imam al-Nawawī ﷺ was unlike other children, for while the other boys played outside, the young Yaḥya often seemed contemplative and was more interested in studying. When he was around the age of eight, some children put pressure on the young al-Nawawī to play with them and insisted so much that he joins them in their play, but al-Nawawī declared: 'I am not created for this!'

One has to appreciate that children are not all the same. Some children are more active and physically inclined, some are more studious and reserved while others are different in other ways. What is important is that all children, regardless of their interests and natural gifts, should be encouraged to pursue whatever they are inclined to as long as it is permissible.

For Imam al-Nawawī ﵀, his interest was in learning sacred knowledge. His devotion to knowledge was so single-minded that he chose not to marry. He felt that his total devotion to studying, writing and teaching would not allow him to fulfill the rights and duties that are due to a wife and family.

Imam al-Nawawī ﵀ completed the memorisation of the Holy Qur'an in Nawā but he wished to complete his studies elsewhere. However, his father needed him to remain in Nawā to assist him in his business. Despite his keenness to study further, Imam al-Nawawī ﵀ believed that the wishes of his parents were more important than his wishes and that he will have no blessings in his study if it is pursued against their wishes. Imam al-Nawawī ﵀ worked for his father for six years and at the age of nineteen, he went to Damascus to enrol in the *Madrasah Rawāḥiyyah*.

HIS QUALITIES

Imam al-Nawawī ﷺ did his best to benefit as much as he could from his studies in this Madrasah. In the first two years, out of the six he spent at the school, he mentioned that he studied for twelve hours per day, and a different subject per hour. In order to remember what he had studied, he taught the subjects he learnt. He reported that his back did not touch a bed for two whole years. He often fell asleep on his arm or dozed off on his books.

«فَلَمَّا كَانَ عُمْرِي تِسْعَ عَشْرَةَ سَنَةٍ قَدِمَ بِي وَالِدِي إِلَى دِمَشْقَ فِي سَنَةِ تِسْعٍ وَأَرْبَعِينَ، فَسَكَنْتُ الْمَدْرَسَةَ الرَّوَاحِيَةَ وَبَقِيتُ نَحْوَ سَنَتَيْنِ لَمْ أَضَعْ جَنْبِي إِلَى الأَرْضِ، وَكَانَ قُوتِي فِيهَا جِرَايَةُ الْمَدْرَسَةِ لَا غَيْرَ».

Imam Nawawī ﷺ says about himself: 'When I was nineteen, my father took me to Damascus. I lived in the school named "*al-Rawāḥiyyah*" and remained there for about two years during which my side did not touch the ground. My only provision during this time was what the school provided and nothing else.'

Time is arguably the most valuable commodity one has. One should constantly reflect on how one uses one's time and find out how to become even more efficient in one's use of it. One should also keep in mind that actions are blessed when they are done in the name of Allah.

«الشَّافِعِيُّ الحَافِظُ شَيْخُ الإِسْلامِ عَلَمُ الأَوْلِيَاءِ، قُدْوَةُ الزُّهَادِ، مُحْيِي الدِّينِ، أَبُو زَكَرِيَّا، صَاحِبُ التَصَانِيفِ، رَجُلُ عِلْمٍ وَعَمَلٍ ... وَقَلَّ مِثْلُهُ فِي النَّاسِ مَنْ كَمُلَ، وُفِّقَ لِلْعِلْمِ وَسُهِّلَ عَلَيْهِ وَيُسِّرَ لَهُ وَسُيِّرَ إِلَيْهِ، مِنْ أَهْلِ بَيْتٍ مِنْ نَوَى مِنْ كِرَامِ القُرَى وَكِرَامِ أَهْلِ القُرَى، لَهُمْ بِهَا بَيْتٌ مُضِيفٌ لَا تَخْمَدُ نَارُهُ وَدَارُ قِرَى لَا يَخْمَلُ مَنَارُهُ... وَأَتَى دِمَشْقَ مُتَلَقِّنًا لِلأَخْذِ عَنْ عُلَمَائِهَا، مُتَقَلِّلًا مِنْ عَيْشِهَا حَتَّى كَادَ يَعُفُّ فَلَا يَشْرَبُ مِنْ مَائِهَا، فَنَبَهَ شُكْرُهُ وَنَهَبَ مَدَى الآفَاقِ ذِكْرُهُ، وَحَلُوَ اسْمُهُ، وَذُكِرَ تَصْنِيفُهُ».

Describing Imam al-Nawawī ﵀, Ibn al-Faḍl wrote: '... The Shāfiʿī Hadith master, the *shaykh al-islām*, the emblem of the friends of Allah, the role model of the ascetics, the reviver of the religion, Abū Zakariyyā, the author of many books, is a man of knowledge and action (upon what he knows)... Few people are like him in perfection; he was granted God-given success in knowledge, as it was made easy for him and readily grasped by him. He was from a family in Nawā, a township known for its generosity and generous inhabitants. They have there a guesthouse whose fire is never put out, and a welcoming place for guests whose signpost never wanes... He came to Damascus to study and learn from its scholars, consuming very little of what it provided for living, so much so that he hardly drank from its water. Gratitude

towards was shown by the people, his mention
reached the far horizons of the world, his name
became sweet on people's tongues, and his
books became highly recognized.'[93]

HIS WORKS

Imam al-Nawawī went on to become the headmaster of the *Dār al-Ḥadīth al-Ashrafiyyah* in Damascus, a post he held until his death. What is truly amazing about Imam al-Nawawī is the amount of books he authored in the mere forty-five years he lived. Despite his short life and the generational gap between him and earlier great scholars, Imam al-Nawawī is hailed as one of the most important scholars in Islam. It is said that he wrote at least fifty texts, dealing with all the Islamic sciences from Hadith, spirituality, jurisprudence to *tafsīr* (Qur'anic exegesis) and the sciences of the Qur'an. He was, and still is, referred to as *Muḥyī al-Dīn* (the reviver of the religion) even though he personally disliked that this title be applied to him, as he did not consider himself worthy of it.

His most extensive work in Hadith is *al-Minhāj fī Sharḥ Ṣaḥīḥ Muslim ibn al-Ḥajjāj,* a commentary on Imam Muslim's collection of Hadith. His commentary explains the chapter headings of Imam Muslim's Hadith collection and provides explanations throghout. His next most important work is *Riyāḍ al-Ṣāliḥīn*, a collection of Propetic sayings dealing with topics relating to spirituality and the believer's inner life. The book consists of fifteen sections covering over 300 chapters on a multitude of issues written in an accessible and attractive manner for both scholars and laymen. One of the most popular and widely read books across the Muslim world is *al-Arbaʿūn al-Nawawiyyah.* This selection of forty-two Prophetic sayings summarizes the main themes and principles around which the religion of Islam revolves, which makes it an absolutely important text that every Muslim household should have. Imam al-Nawawī's ﷺ major work in Shāfiʿī *fiqh* is *al-Majmūʿ Sharḥ al-Muhadhdhab* which he left unfinished. It was completed posthumously by Shāfiʿi scholars in eighteen volumes.

Imam al-Nawawī ﷺ lived at a time of great turmoil due to the Mongol invasion and the Crusades which killed scores of Muslims. Due to illness, he travelled back to the home of his parents in Nawā. He told Ibn Attah, one of his students, to burn some of his writings which he felt still needed more attention and reviewing, fearing that his unchecked and corrected work would fall short of conveying authentic knowledge. After suffering from a short illness, he passed away at his home.

شاه ولي الله

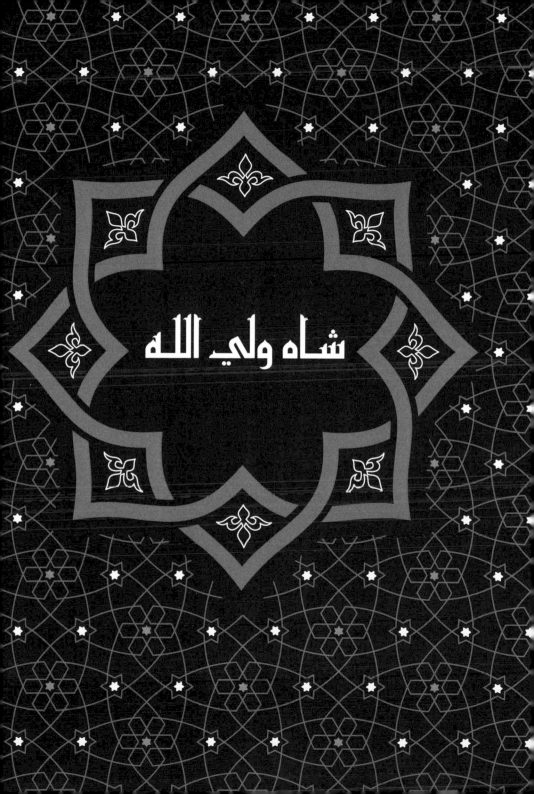

Shāh Walliūllāh

The Role Reviver of Islam in the Subcontinent

INTRODUCTION

SHĀH WALLIŪLLĀH ﷺ (1703-1762) was born at a period which was transitional for the Mughal Empire. His forefathers were among the Mughal elite who played an active role in the state's court and military. His grandfather, Shaykh Wajīh al-Dīn, was a military officer under emperors Shāh Jahān and Aurangzeb. However, he was not just a military officer known for his bravery but also a pious and godfearing Muslim, and this piety and Godfearingness was the hallmark of generations of his family. Wajīh al-Dīn had two sons, the elder Shaykh Abū'l-Riḍā Muhammad and the younger Shāh 'Abd al-Raḥīm. Both brothers distanced themselves from the court and military and pursued the Islamic sciences instead. The younger of the two brothers who had studied under his elder brother as well as other teachers, such as the philospher Mir Muhammad Ẓāhir Hiravī, was acknowledged throughout Delhi as a learned scholar of the highest calibre. He participated in the compilation of *al-Fatāwā al-ʿĀlamgīriyyah,* a comprehensive legal manual to help run the affairs of the state according to the rulings of the *Sharīʿah*. This compilation served as the central legal code during Emperor Aurangzheb's reign. Shāh ʿAbd al-Raḥīm went on to found Delhi's centre for the Qur'an and Hadith, *al-Madrasah al-Raḥīmiyyah*, where he spent his time teaching and leading a relatively secluded life.

Shāh Waliūllāh ﵀ was born in 1114 AH/ 1703 CE in a village called Phulat outside the city of Muzaffaranagar in Uttar Pradesh, India. His educational achievements were remarkable such that he memorized the Holy Qur'an, gained proficiency in both Arabic and Persian and formally graduated from *al-Madrasah al-Raḥīmiyyah* by the time he was fourteen years old. Following his graduation from this madrasah, he sought further knowledge and specialization in the Islamic sciences. At the age of fifteen, he was initiated into the Naqshbandi Order under the supervision of Shāh ʿAbd al-Raḥīm. The following year, his father passed away and the leadership of *al-Madrasah al-Raḥīmiyyah* fell to him.

Shāh Waliūllāh ﵀ dedicated the following twelve years of his life crafting his own methodology in a world where Islam was in a state of transition. He dedicated a significant amount of time to contemplating and reading along with teaching. Ultimately, he had to face up to the same constraints and methodological flaws in

Subcontinental scholarship that his father before him had confronted. The teaching of the Qur'an and Hadith were not given priority in the curriculum. Both Shāh Waliūllāh ۞ and his father felt that the decline of Islam and scholarly tradition in the subcontinent was due to a lack of connection to the main sources of legislation: the Qur'an and Hadith. The study of the Qur'an was relegated to old textbooks and super commentaries which weakened the student's connection with the Qur'an itself. Furthermore, the study of Hadith was very weak in the Subcontinent. Until that point, Indian scholars gave precedence to the study of theology and jurisprudence. In order to complete his understanding of the Islamic sciences, Shāh Waliūllāh ۞ travelled to the Hejaz in 1143 AH/1731 CE. His objective was to gain authorizations (*ijāzah*) in the transmission of Hadith from reputable Hadith masters and broaden his intellectual horizons. In the Hejaz, Shāh Waliūllāh ۞ focused on the study of Hadith and spirituality (Sufism). In the year and a half he spent in the Hejaz, Shāh Waliūllāh ۞, who was twenty-eight, also gained an extensive understanding of *fiqh*. His most eminent teacher there was Shaykh Abū Ṭāhir al-Kurdī who was a strong influence on Shāh Waliūllāh ۞ in all the aforementioned fields. This Shaykh also initiated his disciple into several orders of Sufism. Shāh Waliūllāh also obtained *ijāzah*s from Shaykh Tāj al-Dīn al-Qalā'ī who taught all the six classical collections of Hadith as well as the *Muwaṭṭa'* of Imam Mālik

HIS WORKS

On his return from the Hejaz in 1145 AH/1732 CE, Shāh Waliūllāh ﷺ proceeded to improve his father's curriculum at *al-Madrasah al-Raḥīmiyyah*. His new curriculum no longer relied on old supercommentaries and textbooks but focused on an intimate understanding of Islam's primary sources, the Qur'an and Hadith. Before changing the curriculum, students were generally taught how to recite and memorize the Book of Allah and, in their advanced studies, they studied a commentary of the Qur'an which is specific to their field of study such as scholastic theology or *fiqh*. Shāh Waliūllāh ﷺ stressed the centrality of the Qur'an in his new curriculum. Thus, before specializing in a given field, students had to study the Qur'an in depth and only after an exhaustive understanding of the Qur'an did the students move to the study of other academic fields. Shāh Waliūllāh ﷺ also continued his father's study circle in which he provided his own commentary on the Qur'an to ulema with nothing in front of him except a copy of the Qur'an.

In Hadith studies, Shāh Waliūllāh ﷺ integrated the classical Hadith collections into the curriculum of his madrasah and replaced one of the textbooks with Imam Mālik's *Muwaṭṭa'*. One of his main reform in India was to refocus Islamic scholarship on Hadith studies. Today, schools troughout the Subcontinent still adopt in their curriculum, the reform introduced by Shāh Waliūllāh ﷺ. After the reform he introduced and the initial reorganizing of his institution, Shāh Waliūllāh ﷺ delegated the day-to-day management of the school to his faculty while he turned his attention to writing and addressing the complex problems of the role of Islam in India at the turn of the eighteenth century. The Mughal Empire was an imperial force from approximately 1526 CE to 1720 CE. From the mid-18th-century, the empire witnessed a rapid decline and was eventually dissolved by the British Raj following the Indian Mutiny of 1857. Following the death of Emperor Aurangzheb, who is considered the last independent and effective ruler of the dynasty, in 1707, six emperors ascended to the throne in just thirty-one years. The quick succession of different emperors ended with Muhammad Shāh who ruled for about twenty-eight years. Nevertheless, his administration marked the empire's fall, politically, economically and sociallly.

On the political front, the Mughals were territorially suffocated by emerging empires such as the Marathas, the Sikhs, and the Jats. The court of the emperor also suffered from internal divisions, particularly attributed to cunning powerbrokers within the court.[94] Emperor Muhammad Shāh removed these elements from his court but he was prone to complacency. He was nicknamed Rangila (i.e. pleasure-loving or ever joyous) for his excessive lifestyle. He is notable for failing to repel the Persian invasion of Nader Shāh in 1739 CE. Nader Shāh appropriated the empire's northwestern borders and positioned himself around one-hundred miles from the capital Delhi. Nader

Shāh eventually proceeded to massacre and loot Delhi and reinstalled Muhammad Shāh as a subserviant ruler. He also gained huge support from the Mughal government and annexed key territories in the Sindh and Punjab.

In the economic sphere, Emperor Aurangzheb and his predecessors witnessed an exponential increase in their empire's role in the global economy. The linchpin of its wealth was centralized in Bengal, modern-day Bangladesh. Emperor Bahadur Shāh dismissed Aurangzheb's appointed administrator of Bengal and the region was annexed by the governor of Bihar, Ali Vardi Khan, in 1725. Meanwhile, the British East Asia Company was looking to secure a share in Bengal's wealth. In 1697, the British established a trading port and developed it in 1911 into the capital of British India which they called Calcutta. They increasingly appropriated the wealth and assets of Bengal until the Battle of Plassey in 1757 between the company and Vardī Khan's successor, Sirāj al-Dawlah. With the British occupying Bengal and the Mughal Empire still suffering from the residual effects of Nader Shāh's conquest in the North, the state was on its last leg.

The social condition of the Mughals with its eventual distancing of Islam in everyday life was introduced under the administrations of Emperors Akbar and Jahangir. Akbar gradually shifted his views on religion and philosophy to heterodox ideas. He encouraged religious pluralism to such an extent that he founded his own syncretic and perennialist school of thought known as the *Dīn-e Ilāhī.* Jahangir was also indifferent vis-à-vis religion. And even when Emperor Aurangzheb emphasised the role of Islam in his realm, he could not mitigate the widespread disinterest in Islamic rituals and principles. In contrast to Akbar and Jahangir, the emperors between 1707 and 1738 exhibited poor judgement and leadership which only exacerbated the social decay of Muslims. Many citizens sought excessive luxury and had a lax attitude to moral responsibility. Moreover, Innovative practices, such as the extensive spread of musical instruments, took hold of Muslim communities.

Shāh Waliūllāh's ☙ involvement in the scholarly, political, economic and social activities of Indian society instigated a revival of Islam. In fact, major scholarly schools today claim to be the intellectual heirs of Waliūllāh.

Shāh Waliūllāh ☙ authored a number of works which laid out a vision of orthodox Islam in India that is admired by both scholars and laymen. Two of his primary works in the field of Qur'anic studies are: *al-Fawz al-Kabīr* and *Fatḥ al-Raḥmān fī Tarjamat al-Qur'ān*. In *al-Fawz al-Kabīr* (The Great Victory), Waliūllāh outlined what he sees as the principles of Qur'anic exegesis (*tafsīr*). The book's conciseness made it a key reference for numerous institutions that focus on the study of Qur'anic sciences. *Fatḥ al-Raḥmān fī Tarjamat al-Qur'ān* is Waliūllāh's ☙ translation of the Qur'an into Persian. Persian was still the official language of the court during the Mughal era. The Subcontinent benefited immensely from this simple translation which reinforced Waliūllāh's close affinity with the original message of the Qur'an. His main work is undoubtedly *Ḥujjatullāh al-Bālighah* (God's

Conclusive Proof). This book is a multidisciplinary proof, for the authenticity of Islam gleamed from Islamic sources. The work is regarded as one of the most brilliant synthesis of Islamic scholarship and is taught in prestigious seminaries across the Muslim world.

Shāh Waliūllāh ﷬ was also immensely concerned with preserving the morality of Islam among the Muslims of India. As the Maratha Empire suffocated Delhi, Shāh Waliūllāh wrote to Aḥmad Shāh Durrānī, the Sultan of Afghanistan, soliciting his help and emphasising the unity of all Muslims and the Sultan obliged. Durrānī's forces defeated the Marathas at the third Battle of Panipat in 1761, ending their capture of Muslim lands. However, Waliūllāh continuously pointed out throughout his life that Islam was a minority religion in India and Muslims needed educational reform more than political safeguards. He propagated a vision of Islam in India that was anchored in educating the masses, for in his view "Muslim" was not just a religious classification but also an ethno-nationalist one. This meant a total revamp of society's economic structure which targeted illicit and unjust policies. Shāh Waliūllāh ﷬ also preached about the conflict between home life and professional life, arguing for a practical recommitment to integrating Islamic morality in all spheres of life.

HIS DEATH

Shāh Waliūllāh ﷬ passed away in 1176 AH/1762 CE at the age of 63. His life and works served as a role model due to his incredible intellectual acumen which laid the foundation for subsequent Islamic rebellions in India against colonial powers in the 1900s and also for revivalist movements from that period onward. His work is admired across the Muslim world and is highly praised for its depth and analysis of Islamic sources and modernity.

مولانا انور
شاه كشميري

Mawlānā Anwar Shāh Kashmirī

The Modern Muhaḥaddith

INTRODUCTION

MAWLĀNĀ ANWAR Shāh Kashmirī ﵀ belongs to a rich history of Islam in the Indian Subcontinent. Islam reached the Subcontinent through Muslim merchants who travelled across the Indian Ocean for trade. Islam gained a strong foothold in this region after the Umayyad General Muhammad ibn Qāsim ﵀ conquered areas of the Sindh Province in approximately 93 AH/711 CE. The population responded well to the message of Islam due to its simplicity and indiscrimination between people belonging to different social classes. Several dynasties in the Subcontinent succeeded one another, including the Umayyads, the Ghaznavids, the Ghurids, the Delhi Sultanate and, lastly, the Mughals. After the death of the last effective ruler of the Mughals, Aurangzeb, the British Empire colonised India and subjected its Muslims to intense scrutiny through disenfranchisement and religious and cultural appropriation. By the mid-19th century, the disenfranchisement of Indian Muslims and their increasing lack of connection to Islam reached such an extent that it spurred multiple rebellions against the British. Most notable of these were the campaigns led by Sayyid Aḥmad Shahīd ﷺ on the northern frontier where he was martyred at the Battle of Balakot as well as the Mutiny of 1857 when the ulema led an unsuccessful rebellion against British rule.

These failed rebellions prompted the British to escalate their persecution, imprisonment, torture and even execution of the ulema. This drove the ulema of the Subcontinent to change their strategy from direct rebellion to enhancing their Islamic educational efforts. And so they decided to establish Islamic schools and universities that would attract students and help to preserve the practice of Islam in a society whose governing elites were trying to eradicate it. Some of these institutions were *Dār al-ʿUlūm,* Deoband, and *Nadwat al-ʿUlamāʾ* which served as the educational blueprint for hundreds of subsequent seminaries. Such philosophy of educational empowerment gave rise to one of the most distinguished scholars of the Indian subcontinent: Mawlānā Anwar Shāh Kashmirī ﷺ.

EARLY LIFE

Mawlānā Anwar Shāh Kashmirī was born in Kashmir in 1292 AH/1875 CE in a village called Dudwan. Between the ages of five and seven, he learned the recitation of the Qur'an, the Persian language, Arabic grammar, Islamic jurisprudence and the principles of jurisprudence under his father and Mawlānā Ghulām Muhammad Rasunipura. Mawlānā Anwar said: 'After the age of seven, I did not touch any book of religious knowledge except while I was in a state of minor ritual purity (*wuḍū'*).'[95]

At the age of thirteen, he moved to Hazarah, a district in northwestern Pakistan where he studied for three years. H then decided to join the relatively new Islamic seminary *Dār al-'Ulūm* Deoband, in Uttar Pradesh, India, for further studies. In Deoband, Mawlānā Anwar Shāh Kashmirī became one of the closeset students of Mawlānā Maḥmūd al-Ḥasan, more commonly known as *Shaykh al-Hind*. The latter was the first graduate of the seminary and the principal student of the founders of Deoband, Mawlānā Qāsim Nanotvī and Mawlānā Rashīd Aḥmad Gangohī.[96] In 1312 AH/1894 CE, after approximately forteen years of intensive studies, he capped his achievements by receiving authorization in the classical texts of Hadith such as *Ṣaḥīḥ al-Bukhārī* and *Sunan al-Tirmidhī*. After completing his education in Deoband, Mawlānā Anwar moved to Gangoh, India, where he learned the spiritual sciences of Islam under the tutelage of Mawlānā Rashīd Aḥmad Gangohī.

TEACHING AND THE SHAYKH AL-HADITH

From the outset of revelation, education and learning were highlighted when Jibrīl ﷺ instructed the Prophet ﷺ to read:

اقْرَأْ بِاسْمِ رَبِّكَ الَّذِي خَلَقَ * خَلَقَ الإِنسَانَ مِنْ عَلَقٍ

Recite: In the Name of your Lord who created, created Man of a blood-clot.

Responding to the command of Allah Most High, the Prophet ﷺ assumed the role of an educator as a means to eradicate the injustices of Makkan society. He was aware that the most effective means of social development was educating people as opposed to conquering or subjugating them. Thus, he connected with those he called to Islam through conversation, encouragement and guidance. The revivalists of India adopted the same approach when they failed in their rebellion against the British.

Today, Muslims across the world are oppressed and discriminated against in different ways and degrees. There are a variety of approaches and startegies for resisting such an oppression and discrimination, but the Prophetic model emphasises the importance of religious education before attempting to enact any social change.

In 1326 AH/1908 CE, after spending some time in Kashmir, Mawlānā Anwar ﷺ went to see *Shaykh al-Hind* in Deoband to ask his permission to emigrate to the

Hejaz. *Shaykh al-Hind* persuaded his student to take up a teaching position at *Dār al-ʿUlūm,* Deoband, instead. Due to his proficiency in Hadith, Mawlānā Anwar was tasked with teaching three core Hadith texts in the traditional Islamic studies curriculum: the *Ṣaḥīḥ* of Imam Muslim, the *Sunan* of Imam al-Nasāʾī and the *Sunan* of Imam Ibn Mājah.

At the time, *Shaykh al-Hind* was heavily involved in the struggle for India's political independence from the British. He travelled to the Hejaz to solicit help and support. Before he travelled, he appointed Mawlānā Anwar Shāh Kashmīri as the *Ṣadr Mudarris* (Headteacher) of *Dār al-ʿUlūm,* Deoband. Mawlānā Anwar was also appointed *Shaykh al-Ḥadīth* (Hadith expert) and, as such, started teaching *Ṣaḥīḥ al-Bukhārī* and *Sunan al-Tirmidhī.* In this capacity, he devised his own unique approach to teaching Hadith, particularly *Ṣaḥīḥ al-Bukhārī.* The study of this collection of Hadith was originally confined to the study of contents of Prophetic narrations and their narrators. Mawlānā Anwar Shāh Kashmīrī added depth to the study of the subject by analyzing the chapter headings of *Ṣaḥīḥ al-Bukhārī.* Realizing the huge significance of and relationship between each chapter heading and its content, Mawlānā Anwar Shāh extrapolated Imam al-Bukhārī's personal insight on issues of jurisprudence and theology. This method of studying paved the way for alternative opinions other than those of the dominant Ḥanafī school of thought. Thus, students gained valuable knowledge of the Mālikī, Shāfiʿī and Ḥanbalī schools without missing on the knowledge of the collection's content and its different narrators. This innovative teaching method attracted scores of students who went on to become great scholars in their own right such as Mufti Muhammad Shafī' 'Uthmānī (founder of *Dār al-'Ulūm*, Karachi), Mawlānā Idrīs Kandahlawī (author of *Sīrat al-Muṣṭafā)*, Mawlānā Muhammad Yūsuf Binorī (founder of *Jam'iyyat al-'Ulūm al-Islāmiyyah*, Binori Town), Qārī Muhammad Ṭayyib (chancellor of *Dār al-'Ulūm*, Deoband), and more.

HIS QUALITIES

His first quality was his immense knowledge, which was compared to that of classical scholars. Mawlānā 'Aṭāullāh Shāh al-Bukhārī remarked that the caravan of the Prophetic Companions had passed by but Mawlānā Anwar was left behind. Despite living in the 20th century, his peers maintained that his understanding of Hadith resembled that of the great scholars of the past such as Taqī al-Dīn ibn Daqīq al-'Īd ﷺ and Ibn Ḥajar al-'Asqalānī ﷺ which indicates that it is possible to reach their lofty ranks even today. Like the classical scholars before him, Mawlānā Anwar ﷺ had a phenomenal memory. His son, Mawlānā Anẓar Shāh Kashmīrī related the following:

> He [Malwānā Anwar Shāh Kashmīrī] read Imam ibn al-Humām's *Fatḥ al-Qadīr*, an eight-volume commentary comprising thousands of pages, in

twenty days. He never read it again after that.
Yet, it is well known that he was able to quote
lengthy passages from it, verbatim, decades
later. He also studied the *Musnad* of Imam
Aḥmad ibn Ḥanbal ♨, reading an average of two
hundred pages daily. Despite this quick reading,
he read with concentration, contemplation and
comprehension, deriving evidences in favour
of the Ḥanafī School as he read.[97]

Despite being one of the most erudite and enlight-
ened scholar of his generation, he was always cognizant of
those who helped him fulfil his potential. Mawlānā Anwar
La'ilpūrī, a prominent student of Mawlānā Anwar Shāh
Kashmīrī r, captures well Mawlānā Anwar's immense humility and respect as follows:

After reaching Deoband, my father led me to the
residence of *Shaykh al-Hind*. It was the summer
season and the *Zuhr* prayer had just ended.
There was a crowd of people seated in Hadrat's
[*Shaykh al-Hind*] parlour, surrounding him from
all directions. A person – whose illuminated face
radiated a combined state of light and innocence
and academic (*'ilmī*) grandeur and glory – was
operating the fans which were hanging from
the ceiling, whilst quietly urging people to move
back so that Hadrat would not be discomforted.
My father whispered in my ear, "the person

> operating the fans is Mawlānā Anwar Shāh, the
> headteacher of *Dār al-'Ulūm*."" After hearing
> this my feet fell beneath me [in amazement] at
> how this blessed person – whose academic fame
> was echoing around the world, and who despite
> having his own students in this gathering – was
> busy in the service of his teacher with such
> devotion and reverence (*iḥtirām*).'[98]

HADITH STUDIES AND MIRZĀ
GHULĀM AḤMAD

Mawlānā Anwar Shāh Kashmīrī's ☙ main expertise
in the Islamic sciences was the field of Hadith. He studied
the standard collections of Hadith, learned many other
compilations, reviewed several hundred commentaries,
and wrote commentaries on some of them himself such
as his *Fayḍ al-Bārī*.[99] His perspective as a scholar of Hadith
was that the life of the Prophet Muhammad ﷺ and his
teachings were meant to be publicly disseminated to
defend the Prophet's ﷺ honour, the religion's sacredness
and also to enact social change.

While attempting to enlighten the masses on the life
of the Prophet ﷺ, many Indian Muslims were attracted to
the message of Mirzā Ghulām Aḥmad in the early 20th
century. Mirzā Ghulām Aḥmad was a self-proclaimed
reviver of Islam who claimed to be the prophesised
Messiah at the end of times and that the Prophet 'Īsā ☙

died a natural death. He later claimed to be a prophet of God. He was supported in this by the British who sought to divide Indian Muslims along ideological lines Despite contradicting basic tenets of Islamic belief, Mirzā Ghulām Aḥmad attracted quite a lot of Muslims to his message. Mawlānā Anwar took it on himself to refute his claims and fight his movement. He therefore wrote and lectured on the finality of prophethood, explaining that Muslims who pledge allegiance to any pretender to prophethood after the Prophet, peace and blessings be upon him, have left the fold of Islam. Mawlānā Anwar published several of these texts clarifying the position of Sunni Islam, a position which was included in later constitutions of India.

HIS DEATH

Mawlānā Anwar Shāh Kashmīrī taught at *Dār al-ʿUlūm*, Deoband, for eighteen years. After some internal strife at the seminary, he relocated to Dabhel, Gujarat, India, and taught at the *Dār al-ʿUlūm* there. After five years in Dabhel, he moved back to Deoband due to illnesses. Mufti Maḥmūd Ḥasan Gangohī said:

> *Ḥadrat ʿAllāmah* Anwar Shāh Kashmīrī's abundant study was such that when he had lost the ability to move his hands during his final illness, he would lie down on his side and an open book would be placed on a chair in front

of him. When he finished reading a full page,
he motioned to someone to turn the page.
Ḥadrat would then begin reading
[the next page]...[100]

Mawlānā Anwar Shāh Kashmīrī ﵀ passed away in 1352 AH/1933 CE at the age of 57. He is buried in an orchard on the outskirts of Deoband. His legacy re-emphasized the importance of the pen and speech in contrast to violent methods, even in an era when the land of Islam was fraught with external and internal conflicts. Just as it is important to obtain mastery in whatever one does, it is also important to apply that mastery when necessary. Mawlānā Anwar Shāh Kashmīrī ﵀ used his mastery of the Islamic sciences both in the classroom and also when the faith of Muslims was under threat.

ENDNOTES

1. Narrated by Ṭabarānī, *al-Mu'jam al-Ṣaghīr,* al-Maktab al-Islāmī, 1985, vol, 2, p. 106.
2. Imam al-Dhahabī, *Siyar a'lām an-nubalā',* Mu'asassat al-Risālah, 1985,vol. 5, p. 117.
3. *Musnad Amīr al-Mu'minīn 'Umar*, Dār Ibn Kathīr, 1987, pp. 5-13.
4. Imam al-Suyūṭī, *Tārīkh al-Khulafā'*, Maktabat Nizār Muṣṭafā Bāz, 2004, p. 172.
5. The initial council consisted of 'Urwah ibn al-Zubayr, 'Ubaydullāh ibn 'Abdullāh, Abū Bakr ibn 'Abd al-Raḥmān, Abū Bakr ibn Sulaymān, Sulaymān ibn Yasār, Qāsim ibn Muhammad, Sālim ibn 'Abdullāh, 'Ubaydullāh ibn 'Abdullāh, 'Abdullāh ibn 'Āmir, Khārijah ibn Zayd.
6. Al-Dhahabī, *Siyar A'lām al-Nubalā'*, Mu'asassat al-Risālah, 1985, vol. 5, p. 118.
7. Ibn 'Asākir, *Tarīkh Dimashq*, Dār al-Fikr, 1995, vol. 45, p. 163.
8. Abu Hasan Ali Nadwi, *Saviors of Islamic Spirit*, Academy of Islamic Research and Publications Lucknow, 1971, vol. 1, pp. 15-17.
9. Al-Dhahabī, *Tarīkh al-Islām*, al-Maktabah al Tawfīqiyyah, vol. 7, p. 119.
10. Ibn al-'Imād, *Shadharāt al-Dhahab*, Dār Ibn Kathīr, 1986, vol. 2, p. 41.
11. *Tārīkh Dimashq*, Dār al-Fikr, 1995, vol. 45, p. 213.
12. 'Abd al-Ra'ūf al-Munāwī, *Fayḍ al-Qadīr,* al Maktabah al-Tijāriyah al-Kubrā, 1935, vol. 5, p. 469.
13. *Tārīkh Dimashq*, vol. 72, p. 59.
14. Ibn Abī Khaythamah,*Tārīkh al-Kabīr,* Dār al-Fārūq, 2006, vol. 2, p. 247..
15. Ibn Kathīr, *al-Bidāyah wa'l-Nihāyah*, Dār al-Fikr, 1986, vol. 9, p. 192.
16. Qur'an, 2: 207
17. Yāsir 'Abd al-Raḥmān, *Maws'ūat al-Akhlāq wa'l-Zuhd wa'l-Raqā'iq*, Mu'asassat Iqra' l'l-Nashr wa'l-Tawzī', 2007, vol. 2, p. 30.
18. *Siyar A'lām al-Nubalā'*, vol. 5, p. 136.
19. *Al-Bidāyah wa'l-Nihāyah,* vol. 9, 184.
20. Qur'an, 6:15.

21. *Tārīkh Dimashq,* vol, 45, p. 249.
22. *Al-Bidāyah wa'l-Nihāyah,* vol. 9, p. 210..
23. *Al-Bidāyah wa'l-Nihāyah,* ibid.
24. *Musnad* of Imam Aḥmad, Mu'asassat al-Risālah, 2001, vol. 32, p. 472.
25. *Al-Bidāyah wa'l-Nihāyah*, vol. 9, p. 266.
26. Ibn Sa'd, *al-Ṭabaqāt al-Kubrā,* Dār Ṣādir, 1968, vol. 7, p. 157.
27. *Musnad Abī Ya'lā,* Dār al-Ma'mūn, 1984, vol. 4, p. 326.
28. Ibn Sa'd, *al-Ṭabaqāt al-Kubrā,* vol. 7, p. 162.
29. Ibn Abī Shaybah, *al-Muṣannaf*, Maktabah al-Rushd, 1988, vol. 6, p. 163.
30. Abū Jarīr al-Ṭabarī, *Tafsīr al-Ṭabarī,* Dār Ḥijr, 2001, vol. 24, p. 200.
31. Ibn Qayyim al-Jawziyyah, *al-Dā' wa'l-Dawā'*, Dār 'Ālam al-Fawā'id, 2008, vol. 1, p. 135.
32. *Siyar A'lām al-Nubalā'*, Mu'asassat al-Risālah, 1985, vol. 4, p. 575.
33. Ibid, vol. 1, p. 45
34. Abū Ḥāmid al-Ghazālī, *Iḥyā' 'Ulūm al-Dīn,* Dār al-Ma'rifah, vol. 1, p. 77.
35. Ibid.
36. *Siyar A'lām al-Nubalā'*, vol. 4, p. 585.
37. Ibid.
38. Ibn Abī al-Dunyā, *al-Zuhd,* Dār Ibn Kathīr, 1999, vol. 1, p. 81.
39. Qur'an, 71:10-12
40. *Siyar A'lām al-Nubalā'*, vol. 4, p. 587.
41. *Ṣaḥīḥ Muslim,* no. 2546, Dār Iḥyā' al-Turāth al-'Arabī, vol. 4, p. 1972.
42. Imam Ḥammād traces his *sanad* (chain of transmission) to Ibrāhīm al-Nakha'ī who studied under 'Alqamah who, in turn, studied under 'Abdullāh ibn Mas'ūd the Prophetic Companion.
43. *Siyar A'lām Al-Nubalā'*, vol. 6, p. 400.
44. Imam Bayhaqī, *Manāqib al-Shāfi'ī,* Maktabat Dār-al-Turāth, 1970, vol. 1, p. 92.
45. *Manāqib al-Shāfi'ī,* ibid, vol. 1, p. 94.
46. Qāḍī 'Iyāḍ, *Tartīb al-Madārik wa Taqrīb al-Masālik,* Maṭba'at Fuḍālah, 1970, vol. 3, p. 176.
47. *Tartīb al-Madārik wa Taqrīb al-Masālik,* ibid, vol. 3, p. 177.
48. *Tartīb al-Madārik,* vol. 3, p. 181.
49. In *Tahdhīb al-Asmā' wa'l-Lughāt* by Imam al-Nawawī, Aḥmad ibn Ḥanbal is reported to have said:

وقَالَ أَحْمَدُ أَيْضًا: «مَا تَكَلَّمَ فِي العِلْمِ أَقَلَّ خطأً وَلَا أَشَدَّ أَخْذًا بِسُنَّةِ النَّبِيِّ ﷺ مِنَ الشَّافِعِي».“

'There is no one engaged in knowledge, who has made less errors and held more to the Practice of the Prophet ﷺ, than Imam al-Shāfi'ī.'

50. *Siyar A'lām Al-Nubalā'*, vol. 10, p. 17.
51. Qur'an, 3: 92.
52. *Siyar A'lām al-Nubalā'*, vol. 10, p. 39.
53. Ibn Ḥijjah al-Ḥamawī, *Thamarāt al-Awrāq,* Maktabat al-Jamhūriyyah al-'Arabiyyah, vol. 1, p. 243.
54. See the chapter on Imam Aḥmad ibn Ḥanbal.
55. Imam Bayhaqī, *Manāqib al-Shāfi'ī,* ibid. vol. 2, p. 285.
56. *Saviour of Islamic Spirit*, vol. 1, p. 69.
57. *Al-Bidāyah wa'l-Nihāyah,* Dār al-Fikr, 1986, vol. 10, p. 335.
58. Imam al Jawzī, *Manāqib Imām Aḥmad ibn Ḥanbal* Dār Ḥijr, 2008, p. 243.
59. Muhammad ibn Abī Ya'lā, *Ṭabaqāt al-Ḥanābilah*, Dār al-Ma'rifah, vol. 1, p. 210.
60. *Manāqib Imām Aḥmad ibn Ḥanbal*, p.77.
61. Abū Nu'aym al-Aṣfahānī, *Ḥilyat al-Awliyā'*, Dār al-Kitāb al-'Arabī, 1974, vol. 9, p. 203..
62. *Sunan Abī Dāwūd.*
63. *Siyar A'lām al-Nubalā'*, ibid, vol. 11, p. 324.
64. *Siyar A'lām al-Nubalā'*, ibid, vol. 11, p. 226.
65. Imam al-Dhahabī, *Tārīkh al-Islām, al-Maktabah al-Tawfīqiyyah*, vol. 18, p. 63.
66. Ibid, vol. 18, p. 108.
67. *Siyar A'lām al-Nubalā'*, ibid, vol. 12, p. 393..
68. *Siyar A'lām al-Nubalā'*, ibid, vol. 12, p. 404.
69. Ibid. vol. 12, p. 408.
70. *Siyar A'lām al-Nubalā'*, ibid, vol. 10, p. 85.
71. Ibn Ḥajar al 'Asqalānī, *Fatḥ al-Bārī, Dār al-Ma'rifah*, vol. 1, p. 486.
72. *Siyar A'lam A'lām al-Nubalā'*, ibid.
73. *Tārīkh Dimashq*, ibid, vol. 52, p. 72.
74. *Siyar A'lām al-Nubalā'*, ibid, vol. 12, p. 405.
75. *Siyar A'lām al-Nubalā'*, ibid, vol. 12, p. 466.
76. 'Ali al-Ṣallābi, *Ṣalāḥ al-Dīn al-Ayyūbī.* International Islamic Publishing House, 2010, vol. 2, p. 31.
77. Ibid,vol. 2, p. 31.
78. Stanley Lane-Poole, *Saladin and the Fall of the Kingdom of Jerusalem.* Kessinger Pub., 2007, p. 67.
79. *Ṣalāḥ al-Dīn al-Ayyūbī,* ibid, p 30.
80. Abu Hasan Ali Nadwi, . *Saviors of Islamic Spirit*, Lucknow, Academy of Islamic Research and Publications, 1971, vol. 1, pp. 229–261.
81. *Ṣalāḥ al-Dīn al-Ayyūbī,* ibid, p 32..

82. *Saviors of Islamic Spirit*, ibid, p. 238.
83. 'Abdullāh Nāṣiḥ 'Ulwān,. *Ṣalāḥ al-Dīn al-Ayyūbī,* translated by Khalifa Ezzat Abu Zeid, Dār al-Salām, 2004, pp. 29-33.
84. Bahā' al-Dīn Yūsuf ibn Rāfi' Ibn Shaddāad, *The Rare and Excellent History of Saladin, or, al-Nawadir al-Sulṭtaāniyyah Wa'l-Maḥhaasin al-Yūusufiyyah*, ibid.
85. 'Abdullāh Nāṣiḥ 'Ulwān, *Ṣalāḥ al-Dīn al-Ayyūbi,* ibid, pp. 46-58.
86. *Saviors of Islamic Spirit*, ibid, p. 238. .
87. Antioch is located on the northwestern border of Syria.
88. 'Abdullāh Nāṣiḥ 'Ulwan,. *Ṣalāḥ al-Dīn al-Ayyūbī,* pp. 84-87.
89. *Al-Nawādir al-Ṣulṭāniyyah,* ibid, p. 66.
90. *Al-Nawādir al-Sulṭāniyyah,* pp. 5-10.
91. Ibid, pp. 249-250.
92. *Al-Nawādir al-Sulṭāniyyah,* vol. 1, p. 34.
93. Ibn al-Faḍl, *Masālik al-Abṣār fī Mamālik al-Amṣār,* al-Majma' al-Thaqāfī, 2002, vol. 5, p. 680.
94. Sayyid Ḥusayn 'Alī and Sayyid 'Abd Allāh, the governors of Bihar and Allahabad respectively.
95. *Naqsh-e Dawām Deoband*, Bayt al-Ḥikmah 1996, , p. 108.
96. *Muḥaddith* Khalīl Aḥmad Saharanpūrī, Mawlānā Isḥāq Amratsarī and Mawlānā Ghulām Rasūl were some of his other teachers.
97. *Naqsh-e Dawām,* ibid.
98. *Naqsh-e Dawām Deoband*, ibid.
99. This is a commentary *on Ṣaḥīḥ al-Bukhārī.*
100. Mufti Mahmūd Ḥasan Gangohī, *Malfūẓāt*, vol. 3, p. 232.